PAIN
TO PRAISE

PAIN TO PRAISE

Living Beyond Pain, Bitterness, and Regret

W. Austin Gardner

Copyright © 2024 by W. Austin Gardner

All rights reserved. No part of this publication may be reproduced, distributed or transmitted in any form or by any means, including photocopying, recording, or other electronic or mechanical methods, without the prior written permission of the publisher, except in the case of brief quotations embodied in critical reviews and certain other noncommercial uses permitted by copyright law. For permission requests, write to the publisher, addressed "Attention: Permissions Coordinator," at the email address below.

W. Austin Gardner
austin@austingardner.org

Address
P O Box 469 Ball Ground, GA 30107
+ 770-500-8021

Pain to Praise, W. Austin Gardner —1st ed.

Testimonials

"*Pain to Praise* is a book that dives deep into the power of letting go, offering practical advice and heartfelt stories that'll resonate with anyone seeking healing. Do you want to release the weight of resentment and move forward, unshackled by those chains? I believe this book will help you."

–**Blake Young**,
Missionary to Colombia

"Explore the Biblical practice of forgiveness and its power to impact anyone who practices it positively. Discover how learning to forgive is foundational to following in the footsteps of Jesus. This book comes highly recommended for those seeking guidance on forgiveness and spiritual growth."

–**Chase Southard**,
Missionary to South Africa

"I've known Austin Gardner since 2006. His teaching and guidance have helped me tremendously to deal with my troubles in life; the Lord has used him to help with my biblical answers to my confusions and questions. He has been an answer to my prayers. As a nurse during the time of COVID-19, I saw many people who were intubated, and many people died. I saw Brother Austin in the ICU intubated. I know the Lord is not done with his life. He's not done serving the Lord, even though he has had surgery to remove his cancer for the second time. I know with this book, he will have a great impact on the readers; it will have the same influence he has in my life."

–**Faith Insisiengmay**

"Having been blessed by the author's teachings, preaching, and counseling, I wholeheartedly recommend *Pain to Praise* for anyone seeking to live beyond pain and sorrow. The author has shown in his own life what it means to live according to God's will in the midst of problems and trials. I certainly believe it is worth your time."

–**Gabriel Chedid**

"*Pain to Praise* looks into the Biblical concept of forgiveness through God's abundant grace. 'In whom we have redemption through his blood the forgiveness of sins according to the riches of his grace;' Ephesians 1:7. Salvation and forgiveness full and complete as God always does with a finished work of the grace of God. This message will transform your life."

–**Reverend Hayward Bass**

"I was not a follower of Jesus when I met Austin Gardner. Having grown up a Buddhist, I was quite disenchanted with all religions. However, God used Austin Gardner's teachings to introduce me to Jesus. I can honestly say that my life has changed. The teaching ministry of Austin Gardner has helped me in numerous ways. Austin is genuine, and his teaching is both biblical and extremely practical. I am confident this book will be a blessing and provide assistance on your journey."

–**Lang Insisiengmay**

"Reading Austin Gardner's book *Pain to Praise* has been a genuine gift for me. In its pages, I found practical wisdom about the power of forgiveness and the release of pain and real and touching stories that deeply resonated with my heart. This book offers transformative advice and shows the path to a life of praise and gratitude, even amid the most difficult circumstances. I highly recommend it to all those seeking emotional healing and finding hope in adversity. It is a light in dark times, guiding us toward true freedom in Christ."

–**Lenin Velarde**

"Forgive! A word that's easy to say but hard to practice! My spiritual father, Austin Gardner, has always done it. I have seen it in his own life, towards many of us, in many ways. This book is not a theory. It results from a life of biblical study and reflection on the subject, accompanied by joyful obedience. If you find it hard to 'forgive as Christ forgave you' (Colossians 3:13), you will find encouragement, comfort, and plenty of reasons to do so in these pages. 'The forgiven forgive!'"

–**Miguel Murillo**,
Pastor / Missionary in Peru

"If you have experienced hurt, rejection, and suffering and have chosen to forgive and praise the Lord in the midst of trials, you will find the truths in the book '*Pain to Praise* to encourage and strengthen your walk with the Lord. Embrace the journey from darkness to light with a man God has used greatly for His glory!

–Nate Wilkerson,
Missionary to West Africa

"Embrace the journey from darkness to light with *Pain to Praise*. This book, enriched by the author's wise counseling, has my highest endorsement.

–Sam Paxin,
Attorney at Law

"Working through the process of grief and shame can often be a tedious, seemingly never-ending one. Emotions range on a daily, often moment-by-moment basis. Understanding that pain is something that no one will escape but that we can all have victory over is so helpful and encouraging. Likewise, seeing this process played out in the lives of others who have hit rock bottom and witnessed God lift them from the pits of despair is an extraordinary testimony of His goodness. *Pain to Praise* walks us through Austin's personal journey from brokenness and betrayal to victory and opportunity in the ministry God has for each of us. As illustrated by his personal life and testimony, we cannot control what happens to us, but by the grace of God, we can control how we respond and continue forward for His glory."

–Stephen Underwood

"If you're considering hiking Mt. Everest, it's essential to enlist the expertise of a seasoned guide who has conquered the peak before. In this book, you have the invaluable guidance of someone who has traversed the challenging path from adversity to triumph and from pain to praise. When you find yourself in the depths of despair, facing seemingly insurmountable obstacles, take heart in knowing that others have navigated this terrain. This book serves as a comprehensive roadmap for the journey ahead. Having personally witnessed the transformative journey of the author's life, I eagerly purchased this book upon its release. It surpassed my expectations, and I am confident it will remain a valuable resource for years to come."

–**Trent Coker**,
Missionary to China

Acknowledgments

In the darkest chapters of my life, when life itself seemed almost unbearable, the unwavering presence of my family and friends illuminated my path from pain to praise. My wife, Betty, a beacon of encouragement, stood firmly by my side, her faith in me unshakable. Her unwavering support became my cornerstone, reminding me of our shared strength daily. And my friends, those steadfast beacons of hope who stood by me when the night was darkest, your loyalty has been a priceless gift. Your unwavering support lifted me from the pit of despair and reminded me of the beauty and strength that lie in genuine friendships.

With their unfailing love, our children, Chris and Andria, Stephanie and David, Joy and Jimmy, and David and Katie and their families, called and visited with words of comfort. They sat beside me through my agony, reminding me of the truths I had once imparted to them on brighter days. Their efforts to pull me from despair were heroic, and I am eternally grateful for that. You guys are the greatest gifts God has ever given me. Your love has been my sanctuary, and your faith is my guiding light. And to my friends, you have been a priceless gift.

While many distanced themselves in all the chaos, there were friends (you know who you are) whose loyalty never wavered. In a world where friendships are often tested, theirs proved resilient, offering companionship and a genuine acceptance that helped rekindle my hope in life. Their love and presence were like medicine to my wounded spirit, a testimony to the power of true friendship.

God used each of you to lift me out of the depths and make me capable of helping others. This journey from pain to praise would not have been possible without each of you. I am grateful for your unwavering support, love, and belief in me. Together, we have turned despair into resilience, love, hope, and the transformative power of God's grace.

As a family and alongside my friends, we have lived the biblical truth that the forgiven forgive. We have learned to forgive as Christ has forgiven us, embodying this profound commandment in our daily lives. This principle, this act of forgiveness, has been a guiding light as we navigate the new chapters of life that lie ahead, filled with renewed hope and endless possibilities.

Thank you, from the bottom of my heart, for being the instruments through which God worked His purposes in my life, enabling me to emerge healed and equipped to offer hope and help to others. We are moving forward, embracing the future with open hearts and minds, ready for the adventures and blessings God has in store for us.

W. Austin Gardner

Contents

Acknowledgments..*xi*
Endorsement .... *xv*
Foreword .... *xvii*
Introduction .... *xix*

1. You've Been Hurt…I Understand 1
2. If You Go Down the Spiral… 13
3. Accepting God's Hand 27
4. Stop Thinking About Yourself 35
5. Choose to Obey 45
6. Don't Be a Victim, Be Victorious! 53
7. Control Your Thoughts 61
8. Who Is Being Hurt By Your Hurt? 67
9. Repentance 77
10. From Anger to Gratitude 89

Conclusion *97*
Next Steps *101*
Bibliography *103*
About the Author *105*

Endorsement

Dear reader,

It is with the utmost enthusiasm that I write this letter of recommendation for Austin Gardner. As one who has had the humbling experience of serving as the Senior Pastor of GodsWord Bible Church and the Founder of Crossbridge Marketing & Media, Inc., I have had the distinct privilege of witnessing Austin's exceptional leadership, teaching abilities, and unwavering commitment to the Gospel across both the ministerial and business realms.

In the church, Austin's heart for discipleship shines through Alignment Ministries. His focus on "life-on-life discipleship" has had a profound impact on missionaries and pastors worldwide, equipping them for more effective ministry. His decades of experience – church planting, language learning, and navigating cultural differences – make him an invaluable resource to those he leads.

Austin's prowess as a speaker is equally impressive. As a Certified Speaker with the John Maxwell Organization, he expertly blends biblical wisdom with practical insights that are immediately applicable. His delivery style is both engaging and informative, leaving audiences inspired and equipped. From the business perspective, I've seen Austin's entrepreneurial spirit at work. His understanding of principled leadership and strategic thinking has been instrumental in the success of the organizations with which he has been involved. His ability to translate biblical principles and leadership concepts into a business context is a rare and valuable skill.

Beyond his accomplishments, Austin's unwavering integrity and character set him apart. In both the church and the marketplace, he exemplifies humility, compassion, and a deep commitment to serving others. He is a trusted leader, mentor, and a source of inspiration to everyone in his sphere of influence.

I wholeheartedly recommend Austin Gardner, whether you seek a speaker, mentor, or leader in the ministry or business world. His unique perspective, wealth of experience, and unshakable faith make him an extraordinary asset to any venture.

Sincerely,

Josiah Martin
Senior Pastor, GodsWord Bible Church
Founder, Crossbridge Marketing & Media, Inc.

Foreword

I have known Austin Gardner for almost 20 years, witnessing him and his family endure numerous trials. From health crises to attacks from others, I've seen the heartache that follows these painful situations. But through it all, I've observed Austin's unwavering love for his Lord.

In the middle of the night, I stood beside a man battling cancer, having just had a kidney removed, singing songs of praise to God. I witnessed prayers and praises after Austin emerged from a ventilator, having battled COVID-19 for 21 days. I observed a man leading his family to love Jesus and praise Him amidst family crises. During personal attacks and the distancing of close friends, Austin reminded himself and his family to forgive.

I watched a man walk down the road of suffering and pain, whistling a song from his heart in praise to his Lord. I've been a close personal friend of Austin Gardner and his family; he is as dear to me as any man on earth. I've seen his pain and suffering and, in turn, witnessed his praise.

Austin Gardner has been a support on my own journey. Facing my wife's diagnosis and two of my daughters being diagnosed with the same debilitating disease of muscular dystrophy, I've experienced trials that destroy families and friendships. I've encountered various forms of pain, from people doing wrong to the type of wrongdoing that is seemingly impossible to forgive. Austin Gardner was there for every major crisis in my life, helping me transition from pain to praise.

This book isn't merely a product of someone's writing to sell; it was lived out before it was written. Everyone should take the time to read this book. I empathize with the hurt and pain you may have faced. Looking at this world, it can seem cruel and unfair, with wickedness and wrongdoing. Yet, amidst this, don't let suffering rob you of the joy of praising the God of the Bible. The Lord is too good, too kind, and He will turn that suffering into something glorious. As you embark on this journey, may God place a song of praise in your heart.

Robert and Kelli Canfield

Introduction

If you've opened this book, you are hurting. Whether you sought out this book yourself or whether a loved one gave it to you, either you or someone who cares about you knows that it's time to move out of the darkness and into the light.

This book is for anyone who has been hurt by others and is struggling in a deep, dark pit of pain. The wounds that others have caused you have stolen the joy from your life, replacing it with bitterness and anger. Whether your wound was inflicted months ago, years ago, or decades ago, your pain has begun seeping into every area of your life, transforming who you once were. Not only has your pain interfered with your ability to find joy, but it may have disrupted your relationships with others or even with God. As the brightness in your life dims, your hurt, anger, and despair grow, and you don't know how to stop it.

Yet the fact that you opened this book tells me that you're looking for the light. You know that something in your life has to change, though you may have no idea how to start. You don't want to suffer anymore… You want to heal your wound and begin again.

But part of you may stubbornly refuse to let the hurt go. When you've been hurt by someone, letting go of your anger can feel like letting them off the hook. What happened to you may have been unjust, and you may feel that clinging to your pain is the only path to justice—the only way to gain victory over your aggressor.

I know that feeling well… I come to you not as an all-knowing guide but as a fellow traveler on my own journey of overcoming pain, which I'll share in the pages of this book.

I'm far from perfect, but I have found healing through God, and I want to share what I've learned on my journey with you. My prayer is that this book will help people move from pain to praise… Move out of the darkness and into the light… And move toward the future invigorated by God's unique purpose for you.

From where you're sitting now, you may not believe it's possible to turn your pain into God's glory. But in the pages of this book, I'll share stories of inspiring individuals, both from the Bible and from recent history, who have struggled with pain, just the same as you and me, and not only survived it, but used it to become stronger, wiser, and more compassionate followers of the Lord.

But I understand that some people may put the book down here out of fear, skepticism, or self-sabotage. When you've been hurt, your pain is all you can see. It's like a fog over your vision. Your pain is saying to you, "Put this book down. There's no way you can overcome me. You don't deserve to let me go. You have to carry me around forever."

So if you read no more than this introduction, I want you to read three simple words: God loves you.

Remember these three words, and when you're ready, you can return to this book.

But some of you may be thinking, "I'm ready. I want to know how to overcome my pain."

The journey will not be easy, but I'm here to offer my love and support through the pages of this book—and more importantly, God is extending his hand to you, waiting for you to accept his help.

Your pain does not have to be the end of your story. You can overcome it and find a new beginning.

Join me, and together we can move from pain to praise…

CHAPTER 1

YOU'VE BEEN HURT...I UNDERSTAND

"He healeth the broken in heart, And bindeth up their wounds."
–Psalm 147:3.

In Tracie Miles' book Unsinkable Faith: God-Filled Strategies to Transform the Way You Think, Feel, and Live, she tells the story of a woman named Diane:

"For two years, Diane lived with a man who was an emotionally and physically abusive alcoholic. She finally escaped from the relationship and went to live in a shelter for abused women, but the abuse had rendered her a broken, battered mess, inside and out. Her physical wounds healed, but the invisible wounds from the verbal and emotional abuse lingered, leaving her feeling hurt, resentful, and worthless. She struggled with strong feelings of hatred toward this man who had broken her heart and her spirit. As a result, she became bitter toward all men, even her own brothers. She was afraid to get close to or trust anyone, even God."

If you, like Diane, have been hurt and left with wounds that have taken over every aspect of your life, this book is for you. I myself can relate to Diane's story and have experienced how pain can transform your life and tarnish your relationship with others, even God.

Let's talk…

Someone hurt you, and now your life is filled with pain.

Tell me all about your hurt. I'm not here to criticize, judge, or blame you. I want to understand your hurt so I can help you overcome it.

I've been hurt before. I understand what it feels like to be scared to death, thinking, "God, why have you done this to me?"

I understand what it feels like to be in such great pain that it feels like no one is there for you. But I want you to know that I'm here for you—even through the pages of this book. Though we're not seeing each other face to face, I'm on your side.

The first step we need to take is to get a clear picture of why you're hurting. For some people, this is easy. There was a definite moment when someone did something to hurt you, and it altered the course of your life. For others, identifying the root cause of your pain may be murkier. You may have struggled with anger and pain for a long time without considering where it came from. In your mind, retrace your steps until you find the time in your life when the pain began. Did it begin in early childhood with feeling like your parents didn't give you enough love? Did it begin at school when the other kids were cruel to you? What was your original wound?

Once you've identified the origin of your hurt, reflect on what happened to you. How did it feel? How did you react?

Since then, how has your hurt changed? Is it better or worse than it was before? Some people feel that their pain has increased over the years until it's consumed every facet of their lives. Others may feel that their life is much better now, and they've mostly gotten over their pain—but they're still holding on to anger and bitterness about the past that they're finally ready to let go. Maybe you've tried to just forget or bury your pain, yet you've found this hasn't truly healed you. Where are you in your journey? If your pain was a line on a graph, has it been trending up or trending down over the years?

What's going on in your life now? How does your pain affect you in the present day? What are you struggling with now?

Wherever you are in your journey with pain, there is help for you, and I pray that this book might serve as a guide.

Moving Toward Victory

It's pretty painful to keep thinking about pain, isn't it?

No matter what happened to you or how badly you hurt, you don't want to live there forever, do you?

Even if it may not feel like it, there is help for you... There's a way out...

I want to walk with you on your journey to overcome your pain so you can move on with your life.

It's not an overnight process, but if you take steps toward the light, you can have victory over your pain. You can get to the point where you say, "I hurt, but I will not live my life as a victim of my hurt."

But you may be wondering, "How will I be able to live my life without being a victim of what has been done to me? Won't this hurt stay with me forever?"

I myself have been on this journey before with my own pain and the pain of countless others I've helped as a pastor. You may not feel like it's possible to transform your pain into praise, but I've seen it happen with my own eyes and felt it within my own heart.

You might be reading this book thinking, "How could you possibly understand my problem? It can't be fixed with the kind of simple, stupid solution you're talking about." I understand your concern. After all, pain is personal, and it feels like it has never happened to anyone like you. Maybe you're right, and I don't understand your pain. Let's deliberate... I challenge you as you read the rest of the book to see if you still believe that your pain can't be transformed into praise.

If you're tired of living with your pain, at least give me a chance to help. Throughout the book, you will see scripture that shows us how to overcome our pain. I understand the ease with which you can argue with me, but I believe that our argument with God presents us with a whole new set of problems.

The Choice

I'm hurt. Because I'm hurt, I have bad memories. Because I have bad memories, it causes me to develop a stinking attitude. My stinking attitude causes me to act in such a way that I get more hurt. Unless I take action to stop the cycle, the cycle goes around and around, and the hurt magnifies over time until it's a large, festering wound that destroys my life.

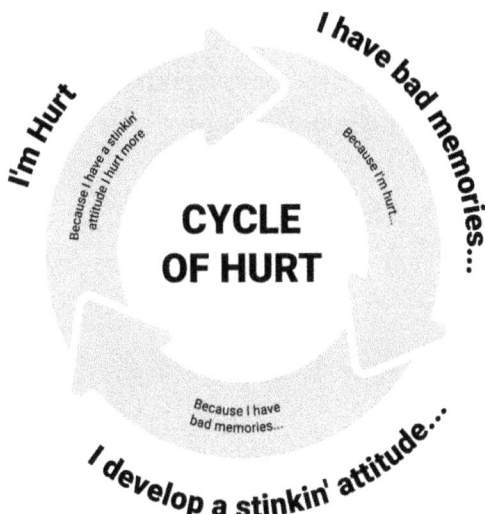

To understand this, we can use the example of a married couple. Over years of helping people through marriage counseling, I've noticed a pattern. Couples will come in wanting a divorce, saying, "We never loved each other." I'll tell them, "You must have loved each other in the beginning… What started this anger?

How did your fighting begin?" Most of the time, these couples can't remember. They've been fighting for so many years that they've forgotten what started their anger towards each other in the first place. They've been spinning around and around the Cycle of Hurt, and their anger towards each other grows. They can either take action to break the cycle, or they can continue to get angrier at each other and watch as the marriage falls apart.

The cycle of hurt transports us to the pity pit. When you're in the pity pit, you can no longer see the truth. Your pain distorts your vision of the world so that all you see is your angry imagination of what others think and say about you. Alone in the pit, you convince yourself that the world is against you and that you are unloved. Because you believe that no one cares about you, you turn away friends and loved ones who try to help, thinking that they don't understand you or that they have bad intentions. The pity pit only has room for one…

When you're hurt, a downward spiral to the pity pit begins…

Your pain causes you to think bad thoughts, which cause you to do bad things… The bad things you do cause more pain in your life, which leads to more bad thoughts and more bad actions… The downward spiral begins.

A young boy has his feelings hurt, so in pain, he kicks a chair. When he kicks the chair, someone sees and makes a snide remark to him… The boy thinks, "Now two people are against me…I hate them!" In anger, he strikes out at whatever or whoever is near. Again, someone sees and yells at him for doing it. The boy's pain and hate increase, and he continues the cycle of lashing out with bad actions and provoking angry responses from others that multiply his own hate. As the cycle goes on, his actions become worse and worse… If he doesn't take action to interrupt this cycle, it could take him to some dark places in life that are never-ending.

The natural descent of this downward spiral leads to a dark pit where you'll feel like you have no way out.

Notice the word feel. It only feels like you have no way out… Through God, there is always a way out. If you change the way you think and shift from pain to gratitude, you take a step toward the light. Slowly, you can climb out of the pit and begin again.

God said, "These things I have spoken unto you, that in me ye might have peace. In the world ye shall have tribulation: but be of good cheer; I have overcome the world." (John 16:33). God has overcome the world, so no pain is too powerful that it can't be overcome through God…

You now have a choice: will you break the cycle, or will you take one small step towards the light?

Wounds start to fester if you don't make an effort to heal them. If you don't take action now to change your thoughts and actions, your pain will gradually take over your life—if it hasn't already. You can stop this from happening, but you have to make the choice to step toward the light.

God Loves You

Many people who are hurt believe God does not love them. But you have to be open to accept the truth. The truth is not what you feel but what is fact. And the fact is that God loves you. He did not abandon you or forsake you, even if that's what it feels like. In Hebrews 13:5, God says, "I will never leave thee, nor forsake thee." If you feel like He has left or forsaken you, that is just an illusion caused by our pain.

You need to remember that your pain and your story will be used for God's glory. You may be going through hurt in your life, but God still loves you. No matter how many people are cruel to you on this earth, God still loves you. God loves you right now. Even in your despair and anger, he loves you.

Recently, I was accused of being abusive. I felt the need to walk away to protect the ministry. Overnight, I lost most of my friends and many of those under my leadership. In response to the public accusations, my friends were afraid to be associated with me because I was being viciously attacked. The young men who used to rally around our vision, hanging on to every word, and always looking forward to working together all of a sudden fled like darkness does when you turn on a light. People who had repeatedly stated they were family now were nowhere to be found. Even after there was an investigation that concluded there was no evidence that the accusations were true, people refused to associate with me. I was left with no one in my life but my family and a few friends. I left my leadership position in the ministry and was forced to abandon the work I had devoted my life to. I was left totally disheartened, wishing my life was over. Unbeknownst to me, I was dealing with stage 4 kidney cancer that had been eating away at my adrenal glands. The adrenal glands handle stress and anxiety, and one can only imagine the stress and anxiety my body was under and unable to process correctly. That's not an excuse for how I handled my pain, that was just what the doctor said…

I felt more hurt by being abandoned and isolated than by cancer and surgery and all that entailed. I felt like my friends left me at the time that I most needed their love and support.

The false accusations had ruined my reputation in my community and directed undeserved hatred and anger towards me. It felt as though I had lost everything…

My heart began growing more and more bitter. I was in the pit described earlier in this chapter… But I slowly climbed my way out. I remembered that Jesus taught us to love our enemies. In Matthew 5:44, he says, "But I say unto you, Love your enemies, bless them that curse you, do good to them that hate you, and pray for them which despitefully use you, and persecute you; that ye may be the children of your Father which is in heaven."

I began trying to love those who had hurt me and let go of the bitterness in my heart. I had to take the time to say, "Austin, it's not about you. It's about the glory of God. If you forget yourself and trust Him, he will somehow turn this around and make something out of it. Nothing happens to you that's not God-filtered and God-approved." I decided to trust God and forgive those that had hurt me. I began to climb out of the pit...

I promise there is a better day waiting when we overcome our pain and climb out of the pit. Can I ask you to join me on that journey?

Corrie Ten Boom once said, "No pit is so deep that He is not deeper still; with Jesus even in our darkest moments, the best remains, and the very best is yet to be."

For those who aren't familiar with the story of this inspiring woman, Corrie was a Christian who helped many Jewish people hide from the Nazis during the Holocaust. She was arrested and sent to a concentration camp, and she later wrote books about her experiences and her faith.

When Corrie said, "No pit is so deep that He is not deeper still," she is talking about being imprisoned in a concentration camp by the Nazis, enduring one of the most horrific experiences that can happen to a human being... Yet through God, she found hope in her immense pain.

Corrie's strength and wisdom should serve as an inspiration to all of us who are suffering through pain, sitting at the bottom of a deep pit, and losing hope that we'll ever be able to get out.

But we can and will climb out of the pit… The pit is deep, but God is deeper still.

Chapter 2

IF YOU GO DOWN THE SPIRAL...

"For the wrath of man worketh not the righteousness of God."
–James 1:20

You're angry at those who hurt you... and that is understandable. They may have done something terrible and unjust to you.

But your anger makes you strike out at people who are on your side and want to help.

Our attitude affects how we hear what people are saying—for good or for bad. If I'm angry, I don't hear correctly because I'm filtering what I hear through my anger. I call this the Filter of Hurt. I have my arms up in a defensive posture, and I'm ready to punch back because I'm hurt. I don't even hear what my loved ones are saying to me. I automatically take it the wrong way because I have a bad, defensive, or resentful attitude. Someone may have made an overture of love towards me, but I took it as anger. Someone may have said, "I love you," but I hear, "I pity you."

FILTER OF HURT

The Filter of Hurt causes us to hear what we imagine, not what is truly said. If someone says, "I know you're hurting, but you'll learn and grow from this experience," I hear, "You're wrong, you need correcting, and maybe now you'll finally mature into an adult." If someone says, "God allowed this, so it will be okay," I think, "Thank you for reminding me that God hates me, too!"

We can see the Filter of Hurt at work when we're having arguments with our family members. If my wife and I are having an argument, we each hear everything the other says through the Filter of Hurt. If my wife gets tired of the argument and says, "Anyway, what do you want for dinner?", my Filter of Hurt will make me say, "How dare you try to change the subject just when I was winning the argument!"

Or if your teenage son comes home late and you scold him, his Filter of Hurt will interpret everything you say for the next hour as a personal attack. You say, "Do you want milk?" and he says, "Milk! So I'm not allowed to drink soda?"

If the Filter of Hurt can distort even our daily, small conflicts with family members, just imagine how it can distort our worldview when we're dealing with a deep well of pain.

When you see and hear things through the Filter of Hurt, you're only thinking about yourself. If you think, "My parents don't love me," you're only seeing the situation from your own point of view. You may be missing that your parents think they're loving you in the best way they know how and don't know that they're causing you hurt.

The filter causes me to even hurt my most well-intentioned friends because I see all through the lens of self-pity. My depth of selfishness in this moment makes me so resentful that I hurt those who love me most.

In my situation, it seemed like some of my former friends made their income from working in the church and were scared of losing their livelihood and that of others if they were associated with a bad leader. They weren't setting out to attack me—they were trying to protect themselves. Even if their decision to cut me off still wounded me, looking at the situation from their point of view helped me move toward forgiveness.

But I want to make the distinction that not everyone will be able to look at their pain from the other person's point of view.

Sometimes, the other person didn't have good intentions at all. For example, if you're a victim of rape, violence, or abuse, the person who hurt you intended to do evil to you. Please don't believe that you have to justify what they did or empathize with their perspective–they did evil against you and against God. Your journey with pain may look different from others because you have to deal with the knowledge that there are people in this world who want to do evil to others.

But if your pain is not due to a situation such as rape, violence, or abuse, and you're dealing with pain caused by someone who may not have had purely evil intentions–such as hurtful words said by a friend, a family member abandoning you in a time of need, a marital dispute, or a conflict with a parent–it can be valuable to examine the other person's point of view and try to understand why someone did what they did.

Destroying the Peacemaker

> *"Blessed are the peacemakers: for they shall be called the children of God."*
> –Matthew 5:9

> *"Until you're right with God, in this world, you're going to be a troublemaker and not a peacemaker."*
> –Adrian Rogers

When we're hurt, we build walls to protect ourselves, but they end up leaving us more alone and isolated. We think we're protecting ourselves, but we're trapping ourselves in a prison of pain.

My hurt and my anger reject any attempt to try to solve the problem… When my loved ones came to me offering possible solutions to my hurt, instead of being grateful for their help, I was angry with them.

The original problem was between two people, but my anger made me lash out at an innocent third party who truly had my best interest at heart.

Anger gives you a bad attitude. You might be talking to people who love you and want to help you with your pain, but you're angry, so you're telling them they're wrong.

Your friend says, "Maybe you should see the other side of it," but you lash out saying, "No, if you're my friend, you'll take my side." The filter of hurt interrupts the meaning.

Our hurt drives us so deeply into ourselves that we cannot hear any help. We only see others attacking us even though they are telling the truth and trying to help.

Our hurt makes us the smallest of men because we turn inward, and nothing outside of our shrunken self even matters any longer.

When the angry person insults the peacemaker, the peacemaker says, "Well, I'm not going to try to help them anymore," and leaves. You lose the person who was on your side and trying to help you because you push them away in anger. The angry person feels abandoned and alone, which feeds their hurt and anger. "Even my friends don't care about me," the angry person thinks—though he or she was the one who drove the peacemaker away.

You might not even realize you're hurting innocent bystanders with your anger. You can't see what you are doing. You are blinded by the hurt. They are called "blind spots" for a reason, and everyone has them. It takes a special kind of friend to be willing to point out our blind spots and help us see the truth. We also must get to a special place where we will accept the truth, the words, and even the love.

The hurt has turned us into something like a rabid dog. We seem to be under the control of something or someone other than ourselves. We can't see our wrongs because our hurt has blinded us.

If I come home in a bad mood, I won't accept what my wife says, even though I love her and have been happily married to her for fifty years. But if I heard the same thing in a good mood, I might agree with a smile on my face. When I react negatively to her because I'm in a bad mood, she'll get mad, too, saying, "Why did you treat me like that? I didn't say anything bad." I'm never intending to hurt my wife with my anger, and I don't even realize I've done it until she brings it up. To avoid harming our closest and most precious relationships, we need to be on guard against our anger and recognize when we're lashing out at those we love.

Here's an old preacher's illustration for you: A boss yells at his employee. The employee goes home and yells at his wife. His wife yells at the kids. The kids take it out on the family pets. It's a trickle-down effect of anger…

Wrong births wrong. My wrong spilled over into all around me. Everyone takes out their hurt and anger on someone they feel the right to express their anger.

Anger has to go somewhere. Unless we release our anger through forgiveness and gratitude, we'll pass it on to the person closest to us…and the next person…and the next person… Before long, the whole world is full of angry people.

Anger has to be dealt with one way or another. If you don't deal with it and let it go, then it will take hold of you, and you will take your anger out on someone else, maybe even someone you love dearly and don't mean to hurt. If we can't get back at the person who is more powerful than us, we lash out at a less powerful person whom we feel we can control.

The more people we hurt, the more people we think are against us. It creates a reinforcing feedback loop of negativity and destruction that keeps us stuck in our anger.

The man in the example destroys his marriage because his boss has hurt him, which has a ripple effect throughout the family. This man comes home, tired of having been abused and mistreated all day long. His wife innocently loves him, and he starts taking his anger out on her. Then, when she reacts back in anger to him, he'll think, "See, everyone's against me."

Some call this the confirmation bias, which is looking for proof of what we already believe.

It's a feedback loop. All of his fears are being confirmed and magnified. It started with being threatened at work, and now his wife's threatening him.

His teenage son says, "Back off, Dad. Why are you yelling at Mom like that?" "Now my kids are mad at me," the man thinks. "Why does everyone hate me?"

If he shows up to the church and the preacher says anything about being kind to your wife, he thinks, "Somebody must have told the preacher about me. Now they're trying to turn the whole church against me. Everybody's against me. Everybody hates me. My life is horrendous."

This man's hurt has invaded every area of his life.

The Consequences of Anger

In John Bevere's book *The Bait of Satan*, he says, "We construct walls when we are hurt to safeguard our hearts and prevent any future wounds. We become selective, denying entry to all we fear will hurt us. We filter out anyone we think owes us something. We withhold access until these people have paid their debts in full. We open our lives only to those we believe are on our side."

When anger seeps into our lives, there's a spectrum of unintended negative consequences that occur.

Anger can cause us to get our feelings hurt even more than they were before. When we lash out at those we love, they may respond in anger and say things we don't want to hear. The man who is abused by his boss day after day comes home and is rude to his wife, complaining about the dinner she made. He didn't intend to hurt his wife's feelings—he's really mad at his boss—but his anger makes him see everything in a negative light. His wife is furious and starts yelling at him, calling him a bad husband and listing out every mean thing he's ever done to her over the last ten years. This man's wound deepens. He thinks, "Not only does my boss think I'm an idiot, but my wife thinks I'm a bad husband. Maybe I'm worthless after all." This man becomes more hurt and angrier and sinks further into the dark pit.

Meanwhile, his wife and children have no idea what happened at work-they just know they are being hurt by Dad. They start to think Dad is an angry jerk because that's what he appears to be. Dad sees himself as a hurt victim of his boss who is just venting. The blind spot caused by his pain prevents him from seeing how he appears to his family. Others do not see us the same way we see ourselves. People may see themselves as the victim, the survivor, the warrior fighting to stay alive, but others may see them as a horrible, vindictive angry, bitter, abusive person driving even those that love them away.

Our anger can destroy our relationships—sometimes for a day, sometimes permanently. A man has held onto anger his whole life because his father left his mother when he was a child. For years, his anger grows and grows, and his attitude toward life turns sour. When he marries a sweet, loving wife, he constantly projects his negative and angry feelings about the world onto her. The man and his wife don't have any other problems in their relationship—they should have had a happy ending. But because the man holds anger toward his father, himself, and the world, this anger seeps into his marriage and makes his wife dislike being around him. If he doesn't take action to let go of his anger, his marriage could fall apart.

Many angry people drive away friends and family with their anger. Even if you aren't cruel to your loved ones, your anger is like a black cloud hanging over your head that those around you can feel—and nobody wants to be around it. Even if your family and friends love you, they may not want to spend time with you when they could be spending time with people who exude gratitude and joy. Gradually, relationships grow distant and crumble, and the angry person wonders, "Why is nobody here for me?"

In the same way they don't see the pain we're going through, we can't see their pain–even when we may be inflicting it. We all know our own intentions, but we only see the actions of others. If our actions are negative and hurtful, that's all others see, even if that's not what we intended.

The most serious consequence of anger is violence. If you look at any horrific act of violence in the news, the root cause is probably anger. The people who commit these acts have sunk to the bottom of the pit and see no hope in life. Their wound has become so deep and all-consuming that they are capable of hurting or killing another human being.

If you look at the history of America, you'll find that, as recently as two hundred years ago, dueling was a common practice to settle disputes. If someone said something rude to you, you could challenge them to a duel and shoot them to death.

Though most of us don't do so through violent acts, the "get even" mentality of dueling is still the way most people handle conflict. We believe, "He hurt my feelings... It's my right to get even." But as we hold onto anger and try to "get even," we hurt those around us. In the old days, dying in a duel over an argument would ruin the lives of your wife, children, family, and friends. Today, our negativity and anger ruin the lives of our loved ones on an emotional level.

In Timothy Keller's book *Forgive: Why Should I and How Can I?*, Keller discusses how the Ancient Greeks didn't see forgiveness as a virtue. They believed that only unvirtuous, "inferior" people needed forgiveness and that virtuous people should look upon those who have wronged them with contempt. Honor was prized over forgiveness... If someone dishonored you by committing wrong against you, the only answer was to get revenge. Forgiving someone was shameful and meant you were weak. Until Christianity, this was the view of the world.

But Christianity introduced forgiveness as strength, not weakness. It wasn't weak to allow someone to dishonor you— forgiveness proved you had moral strength.

Yet centuries after Jesus introduced the concept of forgiveness to the world, most people still live with the old honor-and-shame mindset. Years ago, people enacted this mindset through pistol duels over petty insults. Today, we may not resort to that extreme, but we try to "get even" and hold onto resentment rather than forgiving.

But as the saying goes, "Resentment is like drinking poison and then waiting for the other person to die."

God doesn't want us to "get even." Christianity stands in contrast to the rest of the world by believing in forgiveness. If you're a follower of Christ, disputes aren't resolved by going to a field to duel with a pistol. Nor are they solved by holding onto resentment until the day you can finally "get even." They're resolved through forgiveness.

In *The Bait of Satan*, John Bevere says, "The focus of offended Christians is inward and introspective. We guard our rights and personal relationships carefully. Our energy is consumed with making sure no future injuries will occur. If we don't risk being hurt, we cannot give unconditional love. Unconditional love gives others the right to hurt us."

Our hurt causes us to focus on ourselves and stands in the way of our ability to be good Christians and give unconditional love.

But how do we move past our hurt so we can give unconditional love? Forgiveness.

Forgiveness is the way we prevent our anger from hurting the people we love and slowly poisoning our lives. When we forgive, we can move from pain to praise.

"But how can I forgive?" you may be thinking. "What they did to me was terrible…"

In C.S. Lewis's essay "On Forgiveness," he makes a distinction between forgiving and excusing. When we excuse, we minimize the hurt someone caused us: "Sure, he hit me, but he didn't really mean to do it." We don't need to make excuses for sinful actions—they're wrong, plain and simple. Forgiving isn't excusing. Forgiving is saying, "Yes, he did something cruel to me. There's no excuse for what he did, and he shouldn't have done it. But I'm going to choose to let go of my anger towards him and move on."

If we could excuse people's actions, coming up with reasons for why they "didn't really mean" to hurt us or why "what they did wasn't that bad," forgiving would be easier. It's much easier to forgive someone who didn't really mean to hurt you than someone who intended to do you harm. But Jesus challenges us to have the moral strength to forgive even when someone has evil intentions toward us.

Forgiving isn't about excusing the perpetrator or letting them off the hook–it's about the victim letting go of anger before its poison seeps into every area of their life.

Chapter 3

ACCEPTING GOD'S HAND

"Pride goeth before destruction, And a haughty spirit before a fall."
—**Proverbs 16:18.**

In the last two chapters, we covered how pain can drag you to the bottom of a pit. If you've reached that dark, hopeless pit, how do you get out and climb toward the light?

You need to accept God's hand and let him help you out.

That reminds me of a story…

When I was a boy, I lived on a creek and swam all the time. I went off to a camp for boys during the summer, and they wouldn't let you swim in the deep end if you couldn't swim from one side of the pool to the other. I just took off running, dove in, and with enough momentum and a little bit of swimming, I made it to the other side. They let me swim in the deep end. But I was swimming one day and got tired and couldn't get out. I was dog paddling, scared to death because I couldn't make it to the edge of the pool.

Someone walked along the edge and said, "Hey, Austin, do you need help?" I said, "No."

This happened three or four more times as people passed the pool and saw me struggling. Finally, the fifth time someone came by and asked if I needed help, I said yes. But at first, my pride wouldn't let me admit I needed help.

Your reaction to the first two chapters of this book might have been, "This book might help somebody else, but it won't help me because I don't have that problem."

You may be thinking something like, "I don't need help because I didn't do anything wrong here. Someone has done something to me, and I'm the victim here. If I need help, I just need you to beat them up for me… It's not that I've got a bad attitude. It's not that I'm not forgiving. I'm not bitter. I'm just angry with the way they've treated me."

You're doggy paddling in the pool, hoping you can make it to the other side. How much longer can you last before you accept the hand in front of you? Are you desperate enough yet?

If you make the choice to forgive, you can stop the downward spiral.

But if you choose to not forgive, because you're hurt, you'll strike out and hurt other people. Every time you do that, you're making a choice. You keep making a choice to strike out and get even, rejoicing over others' failures, because you think it's not fair that you're the one hurting.

But I'm here, standing at the edge of the pool, extending my hand to you. I am still wet and dripping because I just got pulled out myself. In the rest of this book, I want to help you overcome your anger and hurt. You may not think you need help—I know because I've been in your position before. But releasing your hurt is a tough battle to go through alone.

Will you accept my hand? Or will you keep swimming until you sink?

And even if you don't accept my hand, someone else, someone much more powerful, is extending his hand, too.

God is extending his hand to you.

Will you accept God's hand and let him help you with your hurt?

> Adam and Eve sin. They know that the day they sin, they're going to be separated from God. But instead of looking for God, apologizing, and seeking forgiveness, they cover up their own nakedness. They don't expect God to forgive–they expect him to punish them with death and destruction.
>
> Then, God comes walking in the garden, and he says, "Adam, where are you?" Adam says, "Well, we're naked and we're ashamed."
>
> God, instead of coming in bitterness and anger for what they did, forgave them. Skins were placed on them to cover them.

Adam realizes, "I found what I wasn't looking for. I didn't want to get help. I wanted to take care of my own problem. I couldn't take care of my own problem. But God loved me so much that God came to me, found me, and provided what I needed."

God meets our needs, but we have to be open to accepting help. We have to recognize that everything we have is a result of God's love—it's not up to us.

When Adam and Eve were hurting and couldn't help themselves, God didn't condemn them. He came to them to forgive. They knew they messed up, and they didn't need God to say, "You're so dumb. Didn't I tell you not to do that?" They needed God to forgive them and provide for their needs. God doesn't condemn us for our sins… Instead, he offers himself as a sacrifice for our sins. He is our substitute, taking our place and suffering the consequences of our sins.

But even though God is merciful and forgiving, humans love to shift the blame for their sins… Adam said, "It's not my fault. That woman made me." And Eve said, "No, it's not my fault, that snake made me." Even as God forgives, Adam and Eve, like so many of us, were unable to accept responsibility for their part in the wrong.

You Are Loved

Sometimes people don't see that they're valued because their hurt is making them interpret everything they hear as negative. When you don't realize that you're valued, it's easy to not value yourself. But you have to choose to accept that you're valued.

When I was hurt, I found it hard to see my value. I forgot that God loved me and was there for me all along. I had to remember that he values me. I had preached these truths for decades, but in the middle of the battle, it seemed like a distant truth. It is so much easier to preach this truth to others than to apply it when you're the one hurting, but I eventually got to a place where I could.

Now consider this same truth for you

God values you. He loves you. He has a plan for you.

Nothing you do will make him love you more, and nothing you do will make him love you less.

You're not a problem in God's eyes—you're just hurting, and you need help.

But you have to choose to accept help. If you want to, you can receive God's help now.

Even if it feels like you're completely alone and unloved, know that God's love for you is always present. He's reaching out his hand, waiting for you to accept it.

Traveling From Pain to Praise

I'm a fellow traveler, and I want to invite you to travel with me from pain to praise…

I've been hurt. I've reacted wrongly. I've thought the wrong thoughts that made me do the wrong things, and they took me further and further into the pit.

I'm not looking at you in judgment. Maybe you're hurting like I'm hurting, and maybe you want some help.

When I was hurt, the clouds covered the sky. The sun went away. The birds quit singing. Life turned dull, dark, and gray, and I didn't know how I was going to go forward anymore. I had no hope. I felt like everyone in the world was against me. I wanted to either die or move to another state where nobody knew me and hide away forever. I wanted any way out I could get. Does this sound familiar at all?

But then I realized that God loves me and that there was a reason for me to be alive. In fact, God was going to take my pain and my story and turn it into his glory and make a name for himself. I want my life to be lived so that God is glorified.

I also realized that my suffering was my preparation for helping others who are hurting. I got cancer so that I could sit with people who have cancer and say, "I understand your pain. We can get through this." I was falsely accused so that I could understand what it felt like to lose everything and use that understanding to help the many lost and broken people in this world. Everything

I have been through, every hurt I have faced, was God teaching me how to help others.

I battle daily to turn my heart from my hurt to the God who loves me. It's a constant struggle, but every day I try to change my attitude about my hurt so I can use it to serve God.

The truth is, you don't get forgiveness until you change your attitude. You have to say, "I'm not going to consider myself a victim. I'm not going to keep whining and complaining. I'm going to react Biblically and correctly to the things that are going wrong in my life."

Take my hand, and let's travel from pain to praise together…

Chapter 4
STOP THINKING ABOUT YOURSELF

As we discuss forgiveness, we must realize that the central problem is that we are focusing on ourselves. We dwell on what happened to us, thinking, "I deserve better!", "Who do they think they are?", "How could God let this happen to me?".

But to forgive, you need to forget yourself. You need to die to yourself and live to God.

Imagine this whimsical scene: as my wife is making cookies, one of the cookies gets angry and says, "I don't like the way I was made." Another cookie is jealous because another cookie is bigger than it is or has more frosting. The cookies are arguing among themselves, saying "It's not fair! What about me?" But they don't realize that their existence is not about them. They're beings created by my wife for a purpose (in this case, to be eaten). It doesn't matter if the cookie wants to be bigger or have more frosting. As long as it fulfills its purpose, my wife is happy. It's not about the cookies; it's about their creator who made them for a purpose.

But the cookies are so self-centered that they're oblivious to the hands that tenderly mixed, shaped, and baked them into existence.

Just like my wife and her cookies, God's hands have shaped us into existence for a purpose. When we focus on ourselves, it's easy to get caught up in petty jealousies or want what we don't have. We want to be taller, richer, more successful... And when we're dealing with pain, we think, "This isn't fair... Why is this happening to me? Why didn't God give this burden to someone else?" But our creation was not about us–it was about what God wanted to do with us. He created each of us for a unique purpose, and when we focus on ourselves, we lose sight of our loving Creator and his perfect intentions for us.

I'm not the center of the universe, and you're not either. God is. It's not about me. It's about Him. I was created by him and for him.

We all live life with the philosophy that "Everything's about me." God owes me a good life, God owes me a healthy life... God owes me, God owes me, God owes me. That's our attitude about everything.

It's so easy for me to think only about Austin...

When somebody hurts me, they don't realize that I'm the hero of my story! You've attacked the main character... I've got to script it so that your move backfires, making sure I end up on top, just like any good hero would. Because in this reality, I'm the important lead, and everything revolves around my happiness and my joy.

It's easy to think this way, but if I catch myself thinking it's all about me, I need to correct myself. I need to say, "Wait a minute. I'm not in charge of the world. I don't ordain events to come to pass. I trust that there's a God Almighty over everything who filters everything that happens to me and is working in my life for his pleasure and his honor and his glory."

Sometimes, we don't understand God's plan for us until the end of the **story...**

> *God looks at Joseph and thinks, "Joseph, I need you to be in Egypt to deliver the nation of Israel so the entire nation and your family don't starve to death." Joseph loves that part of the plan because he gets to be the hero who brings salvation to his people... But he doesn't love the part of the plan where God said, "But to get you there, I'm going to take you through the road of slavery, false accusations, and being thrown in jail and forgotten by your friends, and then I'm going to accomplish my purpose."*

> *Joseph can't fulfill his destiny and be a hero without traveling a road laden with trials and tribulations. He faces the bitterness of life and is hurt by others time and time again. Yet throughout his journey, Joseph realizes that, though those who caused him pain meant to do evil and did not have pure intentions, God turned their evil into good.*

> *If Joseph had let anger and bitterness consume him at the beginning of the story, he would have missed the happy ending—that God put him through those trials and tribulations to prepare him for his destiny. Joseph could not have emerged as a heroic leader without learning from his pain...*

Through pain, Joseph found strength and wisdom. Yet he could only see God's purpose for his pain in hindsight.

Like Joseph, we're unable to see God's purpose for us until the end of the story. What we see as a life-ending catastrophe could merely be the first step in the hero's journey that God has planned for us... Like Joseph, we can learn from our pain and become stronger, wiser, and more faithful by enduring it. Even in the darkest chapters of our lives, God is crafting a narrative of redemption, turning trials and tribulations into stepping stones toward a destiny we might not yet comprehend.

Zoom out to God's view...

You're the size of an ant to God. You're only going to live about seventy to ninety years, and your life is a vapor. We shouldn't even be allowed to say what we're going to do a year from now without saying, "That depends on if God lets me."

From God's perspective, we are all tiny pieces of his plan. We are not the center of the universe. When bad things happen to us, it may not be about us at all.

I do believe in God, and I do believe God is working in my life, and I do believe that God loves me. I'll accept all of those facts...

But when something bad happens to me, I think, "Why'd he let this happen?" And then I have to say, "Wait a minute... That's not about me."

Let's examine the story of David...

David is a shepherd plucked from the fields by God's hand, destined to wear the crown of Israel. But God needs to prepare David for his destiny before he can become king... David is summoned to the palace to sing and play the harp. He goes in and learns his way around the palace. Then, God makes him the armor bearer for Joab, the leader of the army, and in this new role, David learns how to craft battle strategies. David doesn't know it yet, but he'll need that skill when he's king. God then makes David the leader of the army, and David goes out and wins battles and makes a name for himself. He's learned how to make plans, he's learned how to lead people, he's learned how to live in the palace, and he's learned how laws are made.

From his earthly vantage point, David doesn't know what's happening because he sees it from his level, but God is working from above and knows that he's preparing David to be a king someday. God intricately weaves David's narrative, preparing him for the kingship lying ahead.

Then, when David thinks he's somebody because of his success in the army, he has to run for his life. David is chased for years and takes refuge in caves, but finally, the Lord delivers him from his suffering and makes him king.

> *Yet if David hadn't been cast into the wilderness, he would not have learned the humility, dependence, and unwavering trust in God that he needs to be king. He grasps a profound truth: his life is not about becoming king for his own sake. His life is about fulfilling God's purpose for him. Whether God needs David living in a cave or in a palace, David needs to trust that every moment of his life is being used by God to craft his destiny. Through years of suffering, David learns the beauty of surrendering to God's will.*

None of us understand the day-to-day events of our lives now. We can't understand what God is doing in our lives until after the fact.

Because we don't understand God's ultimate plan for each of our lives, when misfortune happens, we say, "Why…why…why?"

I don't understand why God allows some people to get cancer and other people not to. I talked to an old friend of mine I hadn't seen in years who was about the same age as me. I've been dealing with cancer for eleven years, but he has no health issues whatsoever. The first thought that hit my mind was, "What in the world? Why did I get cancer when other people my age are doing just fine?" As human beings, we love the phrase "What about me?" But I suspect that God wants me to use my experience with cancer to help others… I don't know what his plan for me is until it comes into being, so it's pointless for me to say, "God, why are you doing this to me?"

My friend's wife has a form of muscular dystrophy called Pompe disease that will cause her to slowly die. Her two daughters were born with it, too. The odds of two people who were both carriers marrying each other and passing the disease to their children were extremely rare, but it happened. It's easy to look at this tragic situation and think, "Why, God, why? Why would you do this to my friend's family?"

But you must zoom out and say, "What is God doing here?"

> *Joni Eareckson Tada is an American Christian author, speaker, and advocate for people with disabilities. Her life story is one of remarkable faith, resilience, and determination in the face of significant challenges. At the age of 17, Joni experienced a life-altering event. While on a diving excursion with friends, she misjudged the depth of the water and dove into a shallow lake, suffering a spinal cord injury that left her paralyzed from the shoulders down.*

It's easy to look at this situation and think, "Why did God allow this terrible accident to happen?"

But since her accident, Joni deepened her faith in Christ. She became a world-famous author, speaker, and advocate, using her global platform to speak up about both Christianity and improving the lives of disabled people.

If Joni hadn't been paralyzed, she would not have gained the wisdom and resilience she needed to become an important voice in the world. And because people are drawn to Joni's unique and inspiring story of faith and courage, she is given opportunities to share God's message with the world. Without her accident and paralysis, Joni would not be given these opportunities–her story, and the lessons she learned from it, are the reasons people want to listen to her. God used Joni's pain to spread his word. Joni's accident was not the end of her life… It was only the beginning of a beautiful story in which a courageous woman overcame her pain and used her story to help countless others and serve God.

But in order to fulfill her destiny, Joni had to make the choice to accept the task God had given her rather than becoming bitter and asking, "Why me, God?" She chose to see God's hand in her life, and God made her victorious because of it.

Accepting God's Help

The deeper into the pit you go, the darker it gets. The darker it gets, the less you can see the light. The gloomier it gets, the easier it is for the root of bitterness to creep up. But getting that deep will turn out to be your help. Because when you get deep enough and dark enough and realize your helplessness, that's when you accept help and get out of the swimming pool.

No one is going to seek help if they don't think they have a problem. They have to get deep enough into the pit and lose enough to realize, "I need to get out of this, or my life is over."

Paul goes to God and says, "I have this thorn in the flesh and I'm sick. I need to be healed." He asks God three times. On the final time, God says, "When you're weak, I'm strong. When you admit your need, that's when I step in. When you are willing to acknowledge that you've reached the end of the rope, I'll come grab hold of you and pull you up."

But as long as a human being thinks, "I've still got it in me, I can still win, I can still fight through this, I'm stronger than this…" You're pretty much on your own.

But if you get deep enough in the pit, you'll say, "You know what? I can't get out of here. I can't solve this. I don't understand what's going on. Can I talk to you, God?"

But hitting the bottom of the pit doesn't mean you have to wallow there forever before you ask God for help. This choice can happen in an instant. People sometimes fool themselves into thinking that you have to wallow at the bottom of the pit for a long time before you deserve to ask for help. When you're wallowing, you're focused on yourself. We figure, if I punish myself enough, then I'll deserve to get out of here.

Stop wallowing in your pain thinking that somehow, you'll gain enough merit with God for him to like you enough to get you out of the pit.

God loves us so much that he sent Jesus to die for our sins—he already loves you enough to want to help you out of the pit. All you have to do is make the choice to stop wallowing in your pain and accept God's help.

The second I say I need help, God steps in. But I have to say it… I can't go on thinking I can win my battles on my own.

Throughout the Old Testament, God's people want to fight their own battles.

> *In the book of Joshua, the Israelites want to conquer the city of Jericho. But they can't figure out how to get through the Walls of Jericho.*
>
> *God instructs them to march around the walls for six days, and on the seventh day, to march around the city seven times, with the priests blowing trumpets, and have the whole army give a loud shout.*
>
> *The Israelites followed these instructions. As soon as the army shouts, the walls come crumbling down, and the army can enter the city.*
>
> *Joshua and his army got the victory the moment they let go of trying to win it themselves.*

Often, our pride and stubbornness make us want to win our own victories. But if we would only trust in God, we could win the victory immediately.

You can't win the battle alone. Your hurt is going to beat you up. Your bitterness is going to tear your life apart and destroy everyone around you. But if you would just trust God and shout that he's given you the victory before he ever had, you'll have the victory.

To speak of forgiveness without understanding God's master plan for our lives is impossible.

Chapter 5

CHOOSE TO OBEY

"If ye love me, keep my commandments."
–John 14:15

As we have seen, forgiving is moving from thinking of "me" to thinking of God and His will. Once you arrive there, you can move on to think of obeying God. If you are off the throne and He is on the throne, then you are making a decision to obey.

Letting Go of a Record of Wrongs

Love is a choice. It is an act of the will. Keeping a record of wrongs is also an act of the will—a choice not to love—and it is the more natural, easy choice for us to make. It's much easier for us to hold on to resentment towards those in our lives and remember everything they have done wrong.

Picture a married couple getting into an argument. It starts out being about something that happened today, but as the argument progresses, both spouses draw from their records of wrong to bring up wrongs that happened last week, last month, last year, five years ago, ten years ago…

Forgiveness means wiping the record of wrongs clean and starting over with a blank slate. Forgiveness does not mean saying, "It's okay, I forgive you," and then filing away the wrong until the next time you get mad at the person and need to bring up every bad thing they've ever done.

To achieve forgiveness, we need to prevent our tongues from causing trouble by continually bringing up the wrong:

> *"Even so, the tongue is a little member, and boasteth great things. Behold, how great a matter a little fire kindleth! And the tongue is a fire, a world of iniquity: so is the tongue among our members, that it defileth the whole body, and setteth on fire the course of nature; and it is set on fire of hell."*
>
> —James 3:5-6

In R. T Kendall's book *Total Forgiveness,* Kendall shares two ways to control our tongues so they don't interfere with total forgiveness: refuse to point out the wrong to the person who did wrong and refuse to point out the person's wrong to others. Kendall says that we must even avoid pointing out the wrong in imaginary conversations we have in our heads. Doing so only fuels our own anger and doesn't make us feel better. Once we've forgiven, we don't talk or think about the wrong–the record is wiped clean, and we can move on.

Letting go of your pain comes down to two words: choosing and obeying. I choose to obey God. No matter which Christian denomination you come from, we are all taught that we must forgive. We must choose to obey this commandment from God and forgive those who have done us wrong. It's in the Lord's Prayer or Model Prayer: "We forgive those that trespass against us." (Matthew 6:11)

The definition of "choose" is "to decide on a course of action." The definition of "obey" is "submit to the authority of." As believers, we must decide to submit to the authority of God and do what he tells us—which is to forgive. Jesus taught his disciples to pray "Thy kingdom come they will be done."

God said, "If you love me, keep my commandments." In other words, "If you love me, you'll obey me."

Love is a cheap word unless there are actions that go with it. (John 3:18) Love isn't about what you feel, it's about what you do. I told my wife fifty years ago that I love her, and I've been trying to prove it for fifty years through my actions.

If you're a Christian, you know that God loves you and wants you to forgive. (Colossians 3:13) But when it's dark, you can't see the page to read it. You're so beat up, your eyes are knocked black and blue, and you feel like there's no hope. You can't see the truth. But you can see the truth again if you choose to… See the truth that God loves you, that Jesus died for you, and that there is hope. If you just choose to trust Him, obey Him, and forgive those who hurt you, you can get on with your life.

When you're in the middle of pain, you feel like it's never going to end and that there's no life after it. But as time goes by and you look back on it, you may find yourself thinking, "It was terrible, but it wasn't that bad."

But when you're in the pit with your pain, you may not want to forgive. Someone has hurt you, and your anger may be justified.

But remember, it doesn't matter if you want to forgive–God wants you to forgive.

In Nancy DeMoss Wolgemuth's book *Choosing Forgiveness: Moving From Hurt to Hope*, she says, "Choose to fully forgive every person who has sinned against you. This is where the proverbial rubber meets the road. This is where all the tender and wounded parts of your emotions may cry out in self-protection and protest. This is where the enemy will work hard to keep you from going all the way with God and doing what you know you need to do. But this is where you have to go if you want to be free. Choose to forgive each individual (or group) who has sinned against you. Clear their record. Press the delete button. Release them from your custody. You don't have to feel like it. You don't have to want to. But if you want to be an obedient child of God, you've got to forgive."

God calls us to forgive, whether we want to or not...

And forgiveness isn't about letting someone off the hook for what they did wrong. It's about YOU. It's about letting go of your anger and making peace with what happened to you so you can move forward and see the light again. Your best, most vibrant life is on the other side.

You don't forgive for the sake of the offender. You forgive for God and yourself.

Jim L. Wilson said, "Forgiveness is the only way to keep the people that harmed you from turning you into them. The only way to break their control over you and what you think about is to forgive. Is it risky? Yes. Will they wrong you again? Probably… Why should you forgive those who harm you? One answer is so you can be obedient to Christ who commanded you to do it. Another is because it will help you physically, emotionally, and spiritually."

When you don't forgive, it's you that's drinking the poison. It's you who goes to bed at night with negative thoughts running through your head, sleeps poorly, and then wakes up the next morning in a bad mood. Bitterness is like cancer. It eats the host.

I can say, "I don't want to forgive because they hurt me and they deserve to suffer." That may be true… But your hurting isn't making them suffer. It's making you suffer. While you're sitting there whining and crying about how bad you feel, the person who hurt you may have forgotten they hurt you and is living life happy as a lark.

Meanwhile, you're standing in your own way and letting the person who hurt you steal your happiness.

In *Forgiving What You Can't Forget*, Lysa TerKeurst says, "There is a healed version of me that is waiting and wanting to emerge. I am capable of letting go of my proof. Proof only keeps me trapped in the place where the pain occurred, so I keep getting hurt over and over again. I will reject the seduction of nursing my grudges, and I will stop assuming God didn't intervene to help me. Instead of running away, I will run to God when I need help. Perspective is what I'm holding on to and what I'm carrying from here. I have collected the dots. Connected the dots. And corrected the dots. Now, I am choosing to believe God's most merciful outcome is the one I'm living. I'm not a victim. I am a healed woman walking in victory."

Yet, even if you know that forgiveness would help you move on and walk in victory, you still may feel that it's not possible to forgive the person who hurt you…

Obedience precedes feelings. If you do the right thing, the feelings will come. Even if you feel like you can't forgive, forgive anyway and the feeling will come later.

When you say the truth to yourself, you can change the way you think. Speaking truth to yourself eliminates your internal conflict.

Speak out loud, "I forgive _." If you keep saying it, you'll start living it. The power is in the word.

If you're still struggling to forgive, realize that it's not about you, it's about God…

I'm going to admit that God is God, and I'm going to obey Him. I'm going to do what God wants because I love Him and he loves me, and I know he's going to work everything out for my good.

Choosing to obey is a result of realizing I'm not the hero of the story. God is. My life is not for my purposes. It's for his purposes. It's not for my pleasure but for his pleasure.

When I live that way, and when God knows that I am choosing to obey him, he turns my pain into his glory.

Galatians 2:20 says, "I have been crucified with Christ and I no longer live, but Christ lives in me. The life I now live in the body, I live by faith in the Son of God, who loved me and gave himself for me."

We're supposed to be vessels for Christ to live within us. We're supposed to do what Jesus would have done on Earth.

When they were nailing Jesus to the cross, he said, "Father, forgive them, for they know not what they do."

This is the opposite of my instinct, which is to say, "No, they can't do this to me!"

If we are to be vessels for Christ, we need to **forgive**.

> *Decades ago, when my daughter was sixteen and my family was serving as missionaries in Peru, she was raped by three men. When I went to see her in the hospital, I was so angry with these men that I wanted to destroy the entire country of Peru. But when I talked to my daughter, through her tears, she said, "Daddy, Peru didn't rape me. Three wicked men did. Can't you love the Peruvians?" In that moment, I was astonished at how wise my daughter was in spite of her*

youth and her unbearable pain. Something truly horrific had happened to her, and she had every right to be angry. Yet, she found it in her heart to forgive. Years later, she's a wonderful woman and follower of the Lord. Because she chose to forgive, her pain was unable to wreak havoc in her life.

We forgive because we are forgiven. God has given us the ultimate gift of forgiveness for our sins, and in return, we have to choose to obey him and forgive others.

Chapter 6

DON'T BE A VICTIM, BE VICTORIOUS!

"For a just man falleth seven times, and riseth up again: but the wicked shall fall into mischief."
-Proverbs 24:16

You can wallow in pain or not—it's your choice. That sounds unbelievable, doesn't it, after all you have been through? All the pain you felt, the suffering, the accusations, the trauma.

You can continue to be the victim and wallow in your hurt, or you can decide that's not who you want to be. You can think, "Yes, something happened to me that wasn't fair or right, but I'm going to get up and move on. I'm not going to be who I was."

When we wallow, we accept the accusation or the hurtful statements that are made... We think, "They're right... I'm worthless."

If you make your pain your identity, you are choosing to believe that which is not true. You are letting those who have hurt you define you as a victim when God has already defined you.

Remember what the word of God says: you are a child of God, forgiven, accepted, loved, chosen, redeemed, part of the body of Christ. There is nothing that could ever separate you from the love of God. If God is for you, then who can be against you? (Romans 8:31)

God gave His son for us. He is for us. It is God who justifies us. Nothing will ever separate us from him. As Romans 8:35-39 says, "Who shall separate us from the love of Christ? shall tribulation, or distress, or persecution, or famine, or nakedness, or peril, or sword? As it is written, For thy sake we are killed all the day long; we are accounted as sheep for the slaughter. Nay, in all these things we are more than conquerors through him who loved us. For I am persuaded, that neither death, nor life, nor angels, nor principalities, nor powers, nor things present, nor things to come, Nor height, nor depth, nor any other creature, shall be able to separate us from the love of God, which is in Christ Jesus our Lord."

The Bible tells us what your identity is: a child of God. Romans 8:31 tells us that nothing can ever separate you from the love of God.

If you tell me, "Austin, I don't think God loves me anymore," I'll tell you, "That's not possible. Romans 8:31 says you can never be separated from the love of God. Do you want to argue with Romans 8:31?"

God doesn't love us because of how good we are. He loves us because of how good He is.

When we define ourselves as victims, we are accepting the brutality of the bully instead of finding our identity in Christ.

Some people go far enough into the pit that they accept everything cruel that's been said to them, but if they want to leave the pit, they need to say, "That's not me. I'm not going to accept that. I'm going to face what the Bible says is true and what I know to be true. I'm going to accept facts, not just what I feel. I'm going to make a decision to change the way I think and what I do and start the process to get it. I am loved and accepted by God. Nothing can separate me from that love. I'm not going to accept what the bullies are saying to me."

If you're deep in the pit, I want you to look up and say, "They did me wrong, but God allowed it because God has a plan to take my pain and turn it into his glory. I'm going to quit wallowing in it. I'm going to look unto Jesus, the author, and finisher of my faith, and I'm going to believe that he is going to take care of me because he is using me for a purpose. No matter what they've done to me, God will turn it around."

As Romans 8:28 says, "And we know that all things work together for good to them that love God, to them who are the called according to his purpose."

> *Many physically abused people accept the abuse and then pass it on to the next generation. Abused people tend to abuse people.*

If you've been physically abused, I am so sorry that happened to you. That is a horrific type of pain to deal with. But if you want to move on from your pain, you need to look at the bigger picture. God allowed Joseph to be beaten by his brothers, thrown in a pit, and sold into slavery. But instead of wallowing in what happened to him, Joseph says, "I am privileged to belong to God, and I know that God has a plan for my life. I don't understand what's going on here and I don't like what's going on. But I know God is going to do something in my life." God took the bad thing that happened to Joseph and turned it into good.

Where are you placing your identity?

When we're hurt, we make our hurt our identity. We want to wear a sign that says, "I've been abused."

We begin to see everything in our lives through the lens of being the victim. We think, "I must be a bad person because bad stuff keeps happening to me."

But we need to stop and say, "I will trust my identity in Christ. What does Christ say about me? What he says about me is totally the opposite, that I have victory not in me and not in my circumstances, but in Him and in Christ. I have victory over death so that I will end up going to spend eternity with Him. But I have victory over even my painful circumstances because I will come out on top, I will win in the end, and it may be through death."

I have to choose how I think. I have to choose to either think about the bad that's happened to me or about the truth of what the word of God says: one of two.

It's very easy to get into thought patterns that take you down the spiral…

You get what you expect. For example, everyone says the young people of today are no good, but I choose not to believe that. Since I don't agree with that, I get what I expect, and when I'm training young people, God gives me great young people who want to see the world changed and are begging me to help them do it.

If I wake up thinking I'm worthless, when someone looks at me I'll think they're giving me a dirty look, and it'll feed my belief that I'm worthless. When we choose positive or negative thinking, it affects how we interpret what we see and hear in the world each day.

But if I get my head on straight, and I start believing in God, believing that God loves me, believing that God cares about me, and believing that God has a purpose for my life, then I can say, "I don't know what's going on here, but I know God is going to do something big."

When I was in the downward spiral, I did everything I shouldn't have done. I took it to heart. I believed what they said. I thought I was garbage. I wanted to be dead. That made me have a bad attitude and strike out at my loved ones.

But as I was praying and reflecting on my situation, I realized that there was nothing I could do but trust God. I could continue living in absolute misery and make my wife and children miserable, make my grandkids miserable, and make everyone around me miserable. I could walk around with a scowl on my face for the rest of my life, or I could say, "I'm changing."

In the middle of my downward spiral, I decided to change. I decided to turn my attitude around and trust Jesus.

I don't know that I'm all the way out of the pit and back to the top where I used to be, but I'm headed that way.

One day you wake up and realize, "I can't change anybody but me."

You can't make anybody do anything. You can't change how other people feel about you. You can't change what's been said and done. But you can fix yourself.

If I fix my attitude, I fix my thoughts. If I fix my thoughts, I fix my actions. Then, the sun shines again and I can live.

When you make the decision to change, there are three steps you need to take:

Step 1. Admit that you're focused on your pain, not on your future
Step 2. Accept that you can't change anyone but yourself
Step 3. Acknowledge that you need the ultimate help… Ask God to help you change

> *The more you isolate, the more you identify with the victim, and the easier it becomes for your pain to consume you.*

For example, single men with cancer are more likely to die than those with a spouse. People who have hope and support tend to be more likely to beat cancer.

One of the crucial choices you'll face is picking the people you surround yourself with. It's vital to be in a community where forgiveness is valued. Instead of receiving pity or facing harsh criticism, what you truly need is love. Being part of a community that communicates truth with kindness can have a significant positive impact and make a real difference in your life.

For me, after I was hurt, disconnecting from one community to reconnect with another made all the difference in the world. It is hard to reach a victory when you feel shunned by your community. It is hard to forgive when everyone eyes you as the villain. You need the help of another community. Some doors may need to close for others to open.

If we want to beat our pain, we need to stop thinking of ourselves as victims, leave behind communities that don't practice forgiveness, and start looking for love and support in our lives.

Chapter 7

CONTROL YOUR THOUGHTS

"For as he thinketh in his heart, so is he."
–Proverbs 23:7

You are what you think.

When you think there is a problem, you find a problem.

You get more of what you think about. What you think about is where your focus and attention lie.

What does the sign "Wet Paint, don't touch" make you do? It makes you think about touching the wet paint…

Likewise, if you keep telling yourself that you're a victim or dwelling on your hurt, your focus and attention will stay on your victimhood and hurt, leaving you unable to forgive.

In the book Biblical Counseling Keys on Forgiveness, "While you can't control what your offenders do, you can control your thinking about your offenders. God gives us much counsel about what we should sift out from our thinking. Imagine that the

Bible is a "thought-sifter"—a tool that helps us sift the thoughts that should not go into our minds.

Evaluate your thoughts about those who offend you. Remember: Your thoughts produce your feelings."

In the Bible, God instructs us what to think about…

Philippians 4:8 says, "Finally, brothers and sisters, whatever is true, whatever is noble, whatever is right, whatever is pure, whatever is lovely, whatever is admirable—if anything is excellent or praiseworthy—think about such things." In this verse, the Lord is telling us not to dwell on the bad stuff. How could you be a victim if you thought about what is true, noble, right, pure, lovely, and admirable?

Who's in charge?

2 Corinthians 10:5 says, "Casting down imaginations, and every high thing that exalteth itself against the knowledge of God, and bringing into captivity every thought to the obedience of Christ."

Are you controlling your thoughts or are they controlling you?

When we're in pain, it's easy to let our thoughts control us. My inner voice says, "They mistreated you," and I say, "Yes, they did." Your thoughts drag you further and further into the pit.

When a person in the desert is dying of thirst, they see a mirage of water. In the same way, our pain causes us to see mirages. We believe things that aren't true because our thinking is distorted by our pain. For example, someone in pain might think, "No one loves me," but that belief is false-it's just a mirage, only as real as the illusion of water in the desert.

Or maybe their pain causes them to see a mirage that everyone is gossiping about them. At a coffee hour after church, they see two of their neighbors chatting. "They're talking about me," the hurt person thinks, "They're laughing about me behind my back!" Meanwhile, the two neighbors are laughing and smiling about something completely unrelated.

But if you think about the good and focus on the good, you'll find it.

A.W. Tozer said, "The best way to control our thoughts is to offer the mind to God in complete surrender. The Holy Spirit will accept it and take control of it immediately. Then it will be relatively easy to think on spiritual things, especially if we train our thoughts through long periods of daily prayer. Long practice in the art of mental prayer (that is, talking to God inwardly as we work or travel) will help to form the habit of holy thought."

Think on Truth

The devil wants you to think negative things. The book of Revelation 12:10 says, "Then I heard a loud voice in heaven say: 'Now have come the salvation and the power and the kingdom of our God, and the authority of his Messiah. For the accuser of our brothers and sisters, who accuses them before our God day and night, has been hurled down.'"

The devil accuses us, and we accept that truth. But somewhere along the way, I need to lift my shield of faith. "Above all, carry the shield of faith so that you can extinguish the flaming arrows of the evil one. Take the helmet of salvation and the sword of the Spirit, which is God's word. Offer prayers and petitions in the Spirit all the time. Stay alert by hanging in there and praying for all believers." (Ephesians 6:16-18).

In *The Christian Warfare: An Exposition of Ephesians*, David Martyn Lloyd-Jones says, "How do you know, you may ask, whether they are your thoughts or the thoughts of the devil? If you hate them and wish that they were not there, then they are not yours; they are the devil's. He attacks us by hurling evil and blasphemous thoughts at us. He insinuates them. And not only evil thoughts but evil imaginations. It is often very difficult to control our minds, thoughts, and imaginations. The devil has the power to lead them, especially if you are not aware of it and fail to stop him. And thus he will take you captive, and make you intensely miserable."

When negative thoughts assail us, we need to say, "I am going to bring all my thoughts into captivity to Christ. I am not going to just think random thoughts. I'm going to grab ahold of my thoughts and shake them into line and say, we don't listen to or think those thoughts. We think on the right things." When we think about the right things, it shifts our entire outlook.

If women focused on how much suffering it takes to be a mother, we'd have no more kids on this planet. But mothers don't focus on how much pain and hard work it takes to give birth and then raise a child for eighteen years. They focus on the love they have for their child.

If I wake up in the morning and look for something to fight about with my wife, I'll find it. But if I look for something to love her for, I'll find that, too. I need to control my thinking and focus on the good.

In Spanish, when you curse, it's typical to say a phrase that translates to, "That escaped my mouth." The mouth speaks what's in the heart. If your heart is filled with negative thoughts, negative words will escape your mouth. But if you fill your heart with positive thoughts of love and gratitude, loving words will escape your mouth. If I look at my wife and look for things about her to love and be grateful for, sweet and loving words will escape my mouth when I talk to her. "Out of the abundance of the heart, the mouth speaketh." (Matthew 12:34).

If you put into your heart and mind what you want to come out of your mouth, it will come out.

Erwin Lutzer wrote, "Unless you open yourself continually to the work of the Holy Spirit and allow Him to control your thoughts and motives, you too can play into the Devil's hands. Sin will master you and eventually destroy you."

When I'm discouraged, I listen to the wrong voices and think all the wrong thoughts. I focus on myself, not on God.

Make up your mind to think about what's right …Even better, say it out loud to yourself and listen to yourself saying it.

If your inner voice says, "You're a loser," your answer should be, "Well, Jesus said I'm a winner." I can choose to either accept the lie or the truth and what Jesus says is the truth.

You have to defeat the lie with the truth… We must take untrue thoughts captive and bring them into submission to God.

The devil lies, but God doesn't. Yet in our hurt and weakness, we choose to listen to the devil's lies rather than God's truth.

Chapter 8

WHO IS BEING HURT BY YOUR HURT?

"He heals the brokenhearted and binds up their wounds."
— Psalm 147:3

During my time of being hurt, I never intended to hurt others. But I was hurting, so my thoughts were only of my pain, my victimhood, and how I was offended. What I didn't realize was that my hurt was hurting the people I loved the most. Because I was consumed with my pain, I would snap at my friends and family or angrily defend myself to them. I was hurt and badly wanted people to love and understand me, yet when my wife, children, and friends tried to show me love, I responded in anger.

That is what hurt does. It hurts you and it hurts all around you. We must overcome our hurt so we don't ruin our relationships with those we love and continue the cycle of pain.

Let me share a poignant story about a woman who endured the pain of abuse in her past marriage

Her experience with her first husband left her deeply scarred and mistrustful. When she divorced the abusive man and married a loving and caring husband some years later, she found herself unable to shake off the shadows of her past. This lingering fear led her to be overly protective, not allowing her current husband to be alone with their children, as the haunting fear of her past husband's abuse loomed large.

This woman's victim mentality cast a dark cloud over what could have been a happy life with her husband and children. She couldn't allow herself to accept the happiness she now has because the chains of the past still bound her.

She could have found victory by saying, "Bad things happened to me, but with God's strength, I've overcome the pain my abusive ex-husband caused me. Look at my beautiful family and the new life I've built with my second husband, who is a kind man and a good father. I'm grateful that I was able to escape a horrible situation and find a new beginning with a loving husband who treats me well." However, she struggled to release her pain, so she couldn't fully embrace the blessings God had given her.

Unintentionally, this woman's fixation on her hurt begins to affect those around her. She projected her fears of abuse onto her husband, creating strains in their relationship and on his relationship with the children, as she did not let them spend time alone with their father.

One day, the husband found out that his father was dying, and he asked his wife if he could take the children to visit their grandfather and say goodbye.

The woman knew it was important for her children to see their grandfather, but she was unable to join her husband on this trip, and she still didn't trust him to be alone with her children. She refused to let them go with their father, and they missed their final opportunity to see their grandfather before he passed away.

Because the woman had been hurt by an abusive husband years ago, she hurt her new husband, her children, her father-in-law, and her grieving extended family by denying this visit.

The danger lies in the potential for this unresolved hurt to resurface in unforeseen ways. A decade down the road, during a heated argument, the husband may bring up the pain of not letting their kids see his father before he passed away. The unresolved hurt has the power to cast a long shadow over their marriage, threatening the very foundation of their relationship. Moreover, her children may resent her for standing in the way of their goodbye to their dying grandfather.

The lesson here is clear—unaddressed pain has a way of resurfacing and affecting not only the individual but also those closest to them. The path to healing involves acknowledging the hurt, seeking restoration, and allowing the transformative power of God's grace to bring true victory over past wounds.

Hurt people hurt people.

The hurt person is not intentionally hurting others, but they can't see that holding on to their hurt is hurting them and hurting everyone around them.

The pain gets amplified into other areas of life and affects the hurt person's friends and family.

In Peru, there's an emotional tale of a man who, for nearly four decades, found himself not allowed to partake in Christmas celebrations with his family.

> *The reason behind this extended separation traced back to his father-in-law, who harbored deep resentment for the man's marriage to his daughter, a union the father-in-law vehemently opposed and never forgave. The father-in-law would not allow the man to come to his house, so each year, when his wife and kids went to their extended family's Christmas celebration, he had to remain at home.*
>
> *The father-in-law's enduring hurt, stemming from his disapproval of his daughter's choice of a husband, cast a long shadow over the entire family. Imagine, year after year, this man had to face his own children and say, "I'm sorry, but I won't be able to spend Christmas with you because Grandpa hasn't forgiven me." The weight of an old grudge became a barrier, preventing the family from sharing in the warmth of togetherness on the most joyous day of the year.*

This story serves as a reminder of how the choice to hold onto past grievances can ripple through generations. The refusal to let go of bitterness can rob not only individuals but entire families of the precious moments that make life rich and meaningful. In such instances, only forgiveness can reconcile fractured relationships.

Hebrews 12:15 says, "Looking diligently lest any man fail the grace of God; lest any root of bitterness springing up trouble you, and thereby many be defiled."

Notice that we are to look diligently to avoid missing out on God helping us. The grace of God is available to help us when we are hurt, but unless we are careful, we will miss it. When we do, the root of bitterness will cause us trouble and then spread to others. My bitterness doesn't just contaminate me but all around me. It spills out everywhere I go.

I never wake up and think that my hurt is hurting others, yet it does. I never intended to hurt my friends and family, but by focusing so much on my hurt, I did. That is what bitterness will do.

Remember, bitterness is a root. It is small and hidden, so you have to look for it. You have to dig and dig to find that root, and when you find it, you have to cut it out and plant something else in its place. It takes work to root out the bitterness from the deepest depths of your heart.

Roots reproduce if you don't tend to them. They will continue to harm you if you do not plant something else there.

Love needs to take the place of the anger, the hurt, the bitterness.

If love doesn't replace it, a root of bitterness can cause you to hurt everyone around you. Everyone in your orbit is getting hurt because you won't let go of the hurt.

It's like the pot boils over and spills onto the stove and the floor. The stove and the floor were just minding their business… Your pain will boil over and spill on everyone and everything around you.

You may be blind to it. Blinded by your own pain or fear. The deeper in the pit, the darker it is and the less you see. Unless you turn upwards and look for the light at the end of the tunnel, you're never going to get out of it.

There's one more person your pain hurts—yourself.

You may think you're hurting the person who did you wrong but holding onto anger, but you're only increasing your own pain.

In Charles Dickens's classic novel *Great Expectations*, the young protagonist meets Miss Havisham, a wealthy spinster who was left at the altar years ago—and has made this incident her whole life. She wears her wedding dress every day. The uneaten wedding cake still sits on the table, rotting. The clocks in her mansion were frozen at the time she was supposed to be married. She hasn't seen the sunlight in years, and her home is covered in dust and cobwebs. In essence, she let her pain control her life. She even schemes to have her adopted daughter break the heart of the young narrator, Pip, so she can get revenge on men. The sad fact is, that she probably could have found another husband and lived a happy life, but instead, she decided to make her entire life a museum to her bitterness. The man who left her was probably off somewhere with another woman, not thinking about her or what he had done. Though she thought she was getting revenge, she was hurting herself most of all.

It's easy to read this story and think Miss Havisham is ridiculous without recognizing the ways we behave in the same way.

So many people live like Miss Havisham, devoting their lives to feeling the pain of something that happened to them one day years ago. We all have a limited number of years on Earth. Do we really want to waste them in anger and bitterness, frozen in time on the day we were hurt? Do we truly want to make our lives museums to our painful past? Or do we want to give ourselves the gift of happiness and live a joyous life that honors God?

It's time for us to move on and build new lives… There is so much life to be lived if you can just get out of the museum.

If you find that, like Miss Havisham, you've frozen the clock on the moment you were hurt, it's time to unfreeze it and let time move forward again.

Finding Your Purpose

Your hurt is not just hurting you, it's hurting your purpose in life.

Imagine if God looked down and said, "I'm trying to do something through you, Joseph, and Joseph shook his fist in

God's face and said, "I'm not going to listen to you! Go away, my life is terrible!"

That's what so many of us do every day… God has a purpose for us, and when we let our hurt consume us, we're thwarting our purpose.

But if you can find a purpose in the hurt, you can look beyond the hurt.

That's what Joseph does. Joseph looks beyond the hurt to what God wants to do in his life. Because of this, he's able to endure hardship for the sake of fulfilling God's mission for him.

When Jesus was dying on the cross, he looked past his hurt because he knew it would be worth it because he was fulfilling his purpose to save us from our sins.

If you can see the joy past the hurt, you can get out. If you can believe that God has a purpose for your pain, you can get out.

If you dwell on the hurt, you're only going to hurt more and you're going to hurt other people. But if you control your thoughts and try to figure out what your purpose is, you can use your pain for good.

Jesus said to his people, "In this world, you will have affliction, you will have trouble."

The stories in the Bible demonstrate the evil of mankind. All the suffering you can imagine has plagued us throughout history. The hurt and pain we have all experienced have been experienced by millions of people throughout history. This in no way minimizes how bad it is that you were hurt, but I say this to show you that millions of people before you have been afflicted by evil, and millions after you will be, too. As human beings, we're in this together… We all know what it is to suffer.

You're not alone in your pain. Pain is a normal part of the condition of being a human being. You won't be the first or the last person to go through this painful situation, and if you look in the pages of history (and especially the pages of the Bible), you can find stories of people who faced the same type of pain as you, overcame it, and transformed it into something good.

I know you were hurt. I'm sorry you were hurt. It's terrible that you were hurt. I in no way want to minimize how badly you were hurt. But if we dwell on our hurt, we'll never get ahead. Somehow, you have to be strong enough to move on.

Two things can be true at once. The first is that you were terribly hurt, and there is no minimizing or denying the fact that something evil happened to you that should not have happened to you. The second is that if you wallow in your pain, it will ruin your life.

If you do not focus on the pain, you can have purpose and live a meaningful life that honors God.

It takes dying to really live… The Bible teaches that the grain of corn will not reproduce without dying and being buried. The grain of corn dies, it's cast in the dirt, and all of a sudden, it comes alive again. That is what we have to do as believers. We have to realize that what we have been through is horrible, but if it brings us to the end of ourselves, then we can get God's help and begin to live again. When we hit rock bottom as a result of our pain, we can begin again and be reborn, filled with a new purpose to serve the Lord.

We die to be reborn stronger.

Chapter 9

REPENTANCE

"For godly sorrow worketh repentance to salvation not to be repented of: but the sorrow of the world worketh death."
– 2 Corinthians 7:10

James 3:14-18, considering the theme of repentance, sheds light on the transformative power of turning away from earthly wisdom and embracing the wisdom from above: "But if ye have bitter envying and strife in your hearts, glory not, and lie not against the truth. This wisdom descendeth not from above, but is earthly, sensual, devilish. For where envying and strife is, there is confusion and every evil work. But the wisdom that is from above is first pure, then peaceable, gentle, and easy to be intreated, full of mercy and good fruits, without partiality, and without hypocrisy. And the fruit of righteousness is sown in peace of them that make peace."

This verse tells us that our bitter, negative emotions do not come from God–they are earthly and even demonic. We must repent and turn away from these ungodly influences before they corrupt us and cause us to do evil.

On the contrary, divine wisdom, embraced through repentance, is marked by purity, a commitment to peace, gentleness, humility, mercy, fairness, and authenticity. Those who turn to this repentant wisdom become peacemakers, sowing in peace and reaping a harvest of righteousness.

You can't repent if you're still holding on to anger.

Some people want to hold onto their bitterness, hurt, and anger as if they were a prized possession. But you can't repent if you're still holding onto anger.

To repent, you need to change your mind and your actions.

And if you're going to change your ways and let go of your pain and anger, there are three things you need to accept:

1. I realize I've been wrong to hold onto this pain and anger, but now I'm going to let it go.
2. I know God is going to take care of the hurt.
3. I want vengeance. I want to hurt the person who hurt me… But I'm going to let God handle it.

I Peter 5:6-7 says, "Humble yourselves therefore under the mighty hand of God, that he may exalt you in due time, casting all your cares upon Him, for He careth for you."

Turn your hurt over to the Lord and trust in him to take care of it for you.

And if you want to get even… Let God get even…If God wants to get even, God will get even.

A kid walks into a store and sees a jar of candy. The grocer says, "Why don't you get yourself a handful of candy?" The kid refuses to do it. Finally, the grocer reaches in, grabs a handful of candy, and hands it to the boy. As they're walking out, his mother says, "Why wouldn't you reach in there and grab a handful of candy?" The boy says, "Because his hand is bigger than mine."

Why would you take vengeance? God's hand is bigger than yours.

When you take vengeance, you're taking the place of God. When you hold onto anger, you're taking the place of God.

Jesus said, "If you give a cup of water in my name, you did it to me." But then he said, "Saul, why are you persecuting me?"

Saul said, "I haven't done anything to you."

And Jesus said, "When you do it to one of these that are mine, you do it to me."

Every lie, every hurt, and every pain brought against my person that's been against my person was actually against God. Why don't I let him handle it? He's a lot bigger than I am, and he can do it better.

Moving Forward

Repentance isn't just "stop." It's "stop, then start."

It's not enough to let go of our anger… Once we let go of our anger, how will we move forward and start again?

You can't truly turn around unless you're going in a different direction.

If you say you're going to quit holding onto your hurt, but you don't grab hold of something else to do, you're not moving forward. You're going to be worse off.

Repentance involves more than just turning away from sin or letting go of destructive behaviors; it is a profound transformation that includes embracing a new purpose and direction in life.

Repentance begins with a conscious decision to turn away from sinful actions, attitudes, and lifestyles. It's a recognition that certain aspects of our past are incompatible with the life God desires for us.

Letting go of our past involves acknowledging the consequences of our actions, understanding the brokenness they may have caused, and surrendering the old patterns that hinder our spiritual growth.

Repentance is an active and intentional process of change. It's not a stagnant or passive state; it's a dynamic journey of reaching forth toward a new purpose. It goes beyond mere regret or remorse; it involves a commitment to transformation through the power of God's grace. Embracing change means cultivating a mindset open to the Holy Spirit's work in our lives. It requires a willingness to be molded and shaped according to God's purposes rather than conforming to worldly standards.

When we repent, we replace our old, destructive actions with new actions that bring us closer to God, such as seeking God's guidance through prayer, studying His Word, and actively participating in the process of spiritual growth. It's about pursuing a life that aligns with God's calling and design for us.

Repentance allows us to realign our lives with God's divine plan. As we turn away from self-centered pursuits, we open ourselves to discovering the unique purpose God has for each of us. This discovery often involves a deepening relationship with God, listening to His voice, and discerning the gifts and talents He has bestowed upon us. It's an exploration of how we can contribute to His kingdom and fulfill the calling He has placed on our lives.

True repentance means that every aspect of life is directed toward glorifying God. It means making choices aligned with our newfound purpose and consistently seeking God's will in our decisions. It involves continuous growth, learning, and reliance on the Holy Spirit to guide us in our journey. It's not merely a one-time act of saying, "God, I repent," it's an ongoing process of aligning our desires with God's desires for us.

In essence, repentance is a holistic transformation that encompasses both turning away from the old and actively reaching forth toward God's purpose. It's a beautiful journey of surrender, renewal, and the pursuit of a life that reflects the transformative power of God's love and grace.

Philippians 3:13-14 says, "Brethren, I count not myself to have apprehended: but this one thing I do, forgetting those things which are behind, and reaching forth unto those things which are before, I press toward the mark for the prize of the high calling of God in Christ Jesus."

Repentance can be "I'm sorry. I did wrong." But that's not the whole story. It's "I'm sorry and I'm going to start moving in a new direction, toward love, toward God."

To understand the true meaning of repentance, we can contrast the stories of Peter and Judas.

Judas says, "I'm sorry, I did wrong," and hangs himself. That's not repentance. But Peter did Jesus wrong, too, and he repents by following the Lord and doing what's right.

When Peter realized he had denied Jesus, he was overcome with genuine remorse and godly sorrow. His tears reflected a deep sorrow for having betrayed his Lord. His repentance was characterized by a broken spirit and a contrite heart. On the other hand, Judas experienced worldly sorrow marked by guilt and regret. His sorrow was more about the consequences of his actions rather than a true recognition of the gravity of his betrayal.

Despite his failure, Peter sought reconciliation with Jesus. His repentance involved turning back to the Savior, acknowledging his love for Him, and accepting the restoration offered by Christ on the shores of the Sea of Galilee. Instead of turning to Jesus for forgiveness, Judas responded to his guilt by attempting to undo the damage by returning the thirty pieces of silver. His approach lacked genuine seeking of reconciliation with the Lord.

Following his repentance, Peter played a significant role in the early Christian church. His life reflected a transformed and redeemed disciple who, empowered by the Holy Spirit, preached boldly on the Day of Pentecost and became a foundational leader. He turned his pain into praise and aligned himself with God's plan for his life.

But tragically, Judas' response led to despair and ultimately his demise, as he chose to take his own life due to his guilt. He did not experience the redemption and restoration that Peter did. His story serves as a warning about the devastating consequences of worldly sorrow and the importance of genuine repentance.

Emulating the repentance of Peter involves sincere self-reflection, a humble heart, and a commitment to restoration. Here are three steps you can take:

1. **Recognize Failure**

    Like Peter, acknowledge and take responsibility for your shortcomings and sins. This requires honest self-reflection, recognizing specific areas where you may have fallen short or denied your faith. Engage in prayer and ask for the guidance of the Holy Spirit to reveal any areas of your life that need repentance. Psalm 139:23-24 can serve as a prayerful guide: "Search me, O God, and know my heart; test me and know my anxious thoughts. See if there is any offensive way in me and lead me in the way everlasting."

2. **Express Your Contrition and Sorrow**

   Allow your recognition of failure to lead to a deep sense of godly sorrow. Understand the gravity of your actions and how they may have affected your relationship with God and others. Express your contrition through heartfelt prayer. Psalm 51:17 captures the essence of a contrite heart: "My sacrifice, O God, is a broken spirit; a broken and contrite heart you, God, will not despise."

3. **Seek Restoration Through Christ**

   Follow Peter's example by turning to Jesus for forgiveness and restoration. Recognize that true repentance involves not just sorrow for sin but a turning away from it. Spend time in prayer and Scripture, seeking God's mercy and grace. Claim the promises of forgiveness found in 1 John 1:9: "If we confess our sins, he is faithful and just and will forgive us our sins and purify us from all unrighteousness."

Consider sharing your struggles and seeking accountability within a community of believers, such as a trusted friend, mentor, or pastor. The process of restoration is often facilitated through supportive relationships within the body of Christ.

Remember, the key to repentance is a sincere and ongoing relationship with Jesus Christ, acknowledging His grace, and allowing His transformative power to work in your life. The repentance of Peter is not just a one-time event but a lifelong journey of surrender and growth in Christ.

Repentance is saying, "I shouldn't have been thinking about myself. I should have looked forward, believed in God, and done what I was supposed to do. I did not. I've been hurting everyone around me. And I'm very sorry about that. I'm going to stop hurting everyone, but I'm going to do more than just that. I'm going to start loving everyone. I'm going to start filling my heart up not with the hatred that was there before, but with love."

The life of the believer is looking and yearning for the future, and you can't look toward the future while focusing on your past.

In Genesis 41, Joseph forgets the past when he has his firstborn son, and when he has his second son, he becomes fruitful in the land of his affliction. We can't be truly fruitful and embrace God's blessings to us if we are focused on the past.

If you're running a marathon, you can't think about the 26 miles. You have to think about running the next mile ahead of you…and then the next…and then the next. You have to live in the present, focused on God's purpose for you in the current moment.

Forget about your past, focus on your purpose, and change directions. Turn 180 degrees. If you were going north, you need to turn around and go south. You were living in hate. Now I want you to live in love.

If the mother who wouldn't let her kids see her dying father-in-law repented, she would start trusting her family members with her kids and work to repair her relationship with her husband. If the father-in-law who hated his daughter's husband repented, he would invite his son-in-law to Christmas and make an effort to show him love.

You must fill the vacuum left by the hurt when you let it go. And you fill it with the opposite of hurt—love.

James 2:13 says: "For he shall have judgement without mercy, that hath shewed no mercy; and mercy rejoiceth against judgement."

The verse emphasizes the importance of showing mercy to others. As individuals who have received God's mercy, we are called to extend that same mercy to those around us. This involves actively engaging in acts of kindness, forgiveness, and compassion, even to those who may not "deserve" it. Practical application includes forgiving those who have wronged us, helping those in need, and demonstrating empathy toward others.

James 2:13 encourages us to cultivate a merciful attitude in our daily interactions. Instead of rushing to judgment or criticism, we should approach situations with a disposition of mercy. This involves seeking understanding, withholding harsh judgments, and choosing compassion over condemnation. Practically, this means being slow to anger, quick to forgive, and generous in giving others the benefit of the doubt.

James highlights that mercy triumphs over judgment. This underscores the transformative power of mercy in relationships and communities. Practically, individuals should recognize that choosing mercy not only positively affects those around them but also leads to personal growth and a healthier community. By embracing a merciful approach, we contribute to an environment characterized by grace, reconciliation, and understanding.

CHAPTER 10

FROM ANGER TO GRATITUDE

"Not that I am speaking of being in need, for I have learned in whatever situation I am to be content."
– Philippians 4:11

Most people do not think of gratitude as the antithesis of anger, but it is.

Gratitude is rooted in acknowledging and appreciating the positive aspects of life, recognizing blessings, and expressing thankfulness. Anger, on the other hand, often stems from negative experiences, perceived injustices, or frustration, focusing on what is wrong or unfair.

Gratitude tends to be other-focused, emphasizing the kindness, support, or positive contributions of others to our lives. Anger is often self-focused, and centered on personal grievances, disappointments, or perceived offenses.

Expressing gratitude fosters a sense of connection and strengthens relationships. It recognizes the value of others' actions and enhances social bonds. Anger, if not managed appropriately, can lead to disconnection and strained relationships. It may push others away and create a barrier to understanding.

Grateful individuals tend to have a positive outlook on life, seeing challenges as opportunities for growth and finding silver linings in difficult situations. Anger often results in a negative mindset, amplifying the impact of negative experiences and hindering the ability to see potential solutions or positive aspects.

Practicing gratitude contributes to emotional well-being, promoting feelings of contentment, joy, and satisfaction. Uncontrolled anger can lead to emotional distress, contributing to stress, anxiety, and a sense of discontent.

Gratitude operates as a positive force that redirects attention toward the good, fosters connection and contributes to emotional well-being, contrasting sharply with the negative and often isolating nature of anger.

1 Corinthians 10:10 says, "Neither murmur ye, as some of them also murmured, and were destroyed of the destroyer."

In this verse, Paul is cautioning the Corinthians against complaining. The Israelites complained against God in the wilderness, though he had provided them with miracles. God is the destroyer, capable of divine punishment for those who do not accept his will. If we complain, we are betraying God and turning a blind eye to the blessings he has given us, choosing to only focus on what we lack. Because God is more powerful than we can imagine, disobeying him can have serious consequences. We must instead maintain faith, gratitude, and trust in God's guidance.

You have nursed your anger for years. You've thought about the anger until it has consumed you. Now, what I want you to do is to start looking at all the good.

In anger, I see the negative of what happened to me...

But in thankfulness, I see the good...

> *A few years ago, when COVID first began hitting the country, I began having severe headaches and couldn't breathe. I have no recollection of this, but eventually, my family became distraught and called an ambulance to take me to the hospital. It turned out that I had a severe case of COVID. At the hospital, within 24 hours, the doctors told my wife that I would have to go on a ventilator. They put me on a ventilator, where I lay completely paralyzed and unconscious, for twenty-one days.*
>
> *They didn't think I was going to live. They didn't think I'd ever walk out of the hospital. And if I survived, they didn't think I could ever be healthy enough to live a normal life. After twenty-one days, I woke up, and then I spent nine more days in the hospital recovering. I'd lost 80% of the use of my muscles because I'd been lying in a bed for thirty days. And because I was contagious with COVID, my wife and children weren't allowed to see me while I was in the hospital.*
>
> *When I came home, I had to learn how to walk again. It would be easy for me to look at this situation and think, "God, why*

> *did you do this to me?" But instead of anger, I chose gratitude. I chose to think, "God saved me. So many people died of COVID, and I could have been one of them. But God saved me, and I'm grateful to be alive."*

My pain says, "God, why did I have to go through that terrible illness?" But my praise says, "Lord, I am so grateful that I survived that illness."

When you complain, you're praising the devil. When you're grateful, you're praising God. When you complain, you're saying, "God, you didn't treat me fairly. God, you let this happen to me." You're on the devil's side, attacking God, saying, "You didn't do it right."

But when we focus on gratitude, we discover all the ways God has blessed us. I'm so grateful that I lived to tell the story of my experience with COVID because that means God isn't finished with me yet… There's more on the horizon that I get to do for him. I choose to focus on that immense blessing instead of focusing on my pain.

The Attitude Battle

If you don't turn from anger to gratitude, you'll go right back to anger. You have to fight to be thankful… It's a constant battle, and there are enemies of gratitude everywhere.

The first is the comparing game. This looks like, "No fair! Why did I get cancer and my friend didn't?" When we busy ourselves looking at what others have, we fail to be grateful for what we do have. I may have cancer, but I should thank God that I'm alive today to write this book. It doesn't matter that "it's not fair" that others don't have to go through this illness.

Another enemy of gratitude is the complaining game. Complaining is the opposite of praise to God. Want to know how to praise the devil? Complain. Complaining is the outflow of anger. When you complain, you're saying, "God, you haven't done me right, and I am suffering for it."

The way to defeat complaining is to pray and seek God's will about our problems. Rather than complaining about our problems, we should turn them over to God and seek his help in dealing with them.

We're often so focused on ourselves that we're not thankful. Living in gratitude is a constant battle, but it's well worth fighting.

When you've been hurt, you want to crawl into a hole and die. You're down in the deep, dark pit, but one day you wake up and realize, "I've been pouting, whining, and crying long enough. I've been angry, mad, and bitter long enough. It's only painting my world dark and mean and ugly. I can't take it any longer." You turn to God and say, "I trust you. I know that you are in charge of my life and that you brought me through here. I will learn to be content wherever you put me. I'm going to be grateful to you for the life I have, the family I have, and all of the blessings you've given me."

I would like to challenge everyone who is hurting right now to stop focusing on the hurt and start focusing on the fact that you lived through it. You can focus on the fact that you've been beaten down, mistreated, and abused, or you can focus on the fact that God has taken good care of you and helped you survive through the pain.

Out of the pit...

When I was a kid, one of my pastors said, "I want you to pray and only say thank you. Don't ask God for anything. Just tell him what you're thankful for."

I said, "How can I do that?"

He said, "Do you have two eyes?" "Yes."

"Well, then, thank him, because a lot of people don't have two."

Every day, no matter what problems we face, we each have so much to be grateful for that we don't even realize.

When my son found out that he was a diabetic, I tried to help him understand that, though it was horrible, there were others who suffered more.

As Helen Keller once said, "I cried because I had no shoes until I met a man who had no feet."

There will always be someone who has less than us, and when we recognize this, we can focus on being grateful for what we have rather than being angry at God over what we lack.

When we become aware of just how many blessings God has given us, we can push past our pain and move toward the light.

In 2 Corinthians 12, Paul asks God to remove a thorn in his flesh. God answers, "My grace is sufficient for thee: for my strength is made perfect in weakness." Paul then says, "Most gladly therefore will I rather glory in my infirmities, that the power of Christ may rest upon me. Therefore, I take pleasure in infirmities, in reproaches, in necessities, in persecutions, in distresses for Christ's sake: for when I am weak, then am I strong."

God is going to do something massive in your life. He has a plan for your pain... In the future, you may find yourself thanking God for the pain you went through because your experience helped you fulfill God's purpose for you.

God does not waste pain. Though someone hurt you with evil intentions, God knows how to use your pain for good. Through your pain, God may send you to help others or to spread his word. When you get victory over your troubles, you can help others get victory over theirs.

I'm thankful for my hurt because it allows me to help others who are hurting. I can sit across from a man who's been diagnosed with cancer and say, "I know what it looks like to be in your position. Let me help you through this." I can sit across from someone who has lost everything and say, "I've been there, too... There's hope for you to rebuild your life."

I've climbed out of the pit, I've found my purpose in life, and I have overcome the hurt. I've looked to the future, I've left the pain behind, and I've put my focus on helping other people. I'm using my hurt. Instead of wallowing, I'm working. Instead of suffering, I'm serving.

I want to help people get out of the downward spiral in the pit, and I want them to feel the sun on their faces again.

How did God comfort you when you were in pain? How will you thank him by helping others overcome pain?

It's not enough to get victory over your own pain… Once you've done so, you can help others get victory over theirs.

This is how you turn your pain into God's glory and replace your hurt with love.

Conclusion

Are you ready to climb out of the pit?

I hope that as you've read this book, no matter how deep down you have fallen and no matter how dark your life has gotten, a glimpse of the light has caught your eye.

Now, it's up to you to move toward it.

Go on, take your first step. I'm standing here with you, cheering you on, understanding how difficult this first step can be. Even if you're still struggling to believe that you can get out of the pit, I believe in you. Everyone who has ever struggled with pain and climbed out of the pit believes in you. And I bet you have loved ones who believe in you and are ready to extend their support.

But most importantly, someone infinitely more powerful and loving than any of us believes in you… God's guiding hand is reaching down to you, ready to help you climb out of the pit.

Will you take it?

When you're out of the pit, life can begin again. And I believe that life on the other side of the pit can be even sweeter than life was before you were hurt. "How can that be possible?" you might be thinking. But I believe that once you've hit rock bottom and been reborn, you will live the rest of your life with the knowledge that you overcame the worst. You survived the darkness… This knowledge is a source of strength. You can move forward knowing that no matter what happens to you, you have the ability to overcome it—and not only overcome it but to turn your pain into God's glory.

Life on the other side of the pit can be even better because your time in the darkness and your battle to overcome it have helped you realign with God's purpose for you. Now, you can move forward with even more clarity, intention, and gratitude than you may ever have before.

But you now stand at a crucial crossroads: you can move toward the light, or you can continue to sit in the darkness. Wounds that aren't healed fester. And the longer you leave your wound untreated, the more destruction it can rage in your life.

The light is peeking into the pit now, but if you choose to turn away from it, you'll find yourself sinking further into darkness. You need to take the first step now before your courage leaves you.

I pray that this book has provided help to you in your time of need. As someone who has faced my own battle with pain, writing this book to help others was the least I could do to express my gratitude to God and to my loved ones for helping me climb out of the pit.

None of us can face this journey alone.

Next Steps

Follow along with Austin on his journey of faith, and turning *Pain to Praise*. If you'd like to set up a call and talk about your unique situation, connect with the author below.

You can also join his newsletter so you never miss daily encouragement and news from Austin.

http://austingardner.org/

Book Austin to Speak at Your Next Event

https://www.johncmaxwellgroup.com/austingardner

Read up on Austin's Blog

https://www.alignmentministries.com/from-austins-pen

Bibliography

Warren W. Wiersbe, *The Bumps Are What You Climb On: Encouragement for Difficult Days* (Grand Rapids, MI: Baker Books, 2002), 123.

John Bevere, *The Bait of Satan*, 20th Anniversary Edition (Lake Mary, FL: Charisma House, 2014), 261.

Lysa TerKeurst, *Forgiving What You Can't Forget: Discover How to Move On, Make Peace with Painful Memories, and Create a Life That's Beautiful Again* (Nashville: Thomas Nelson, 2020), 100–101.

R. T. Kendall, *Total Forgiveness: When Everything in You Wants to Hold a Grudge, Point a Finger, and Remember the Pain - God Wants You to Lay It All Aside* (Lake Mary, FL: Charisma House, 2010).

Erwin W. Lutzer, *When You've Been Wronged: Moving From Bitterness to Forgiveness* (Chicago, IL: Moody Publishers, 2007).

Nancy DeMoss Wolgemuth, *Choosing Forgiveness: Moving from Hurt to Hope* (Chicago, IL: Moody Publishers, 2022).

June Hunt, *Biblical Counseling Keys on Forgiveness: The Freedom to Let Go* (Dallas, TX: Hope For The Heart, 2008), 5.

Bruce Wilkinson, *The Secret of Lasting Forgiveness: How To Find Peace By Forgiving Others and Yourself* (Zeal Books, March 27, 2018)

Stephen Mitchell, *Joseph and the Way of Forgiveness: A Story About Letting Go* (St. Martin's Essentials, September 17, 2019)

Harriet Beecher Stowe, *Uncle Tom's Cabin (Original Version), by Harriet Beecher Stowe (Redemption Edition)* (May 3rd, 2022)

Gene Edwards, *The Prisoner in the Third Cell* (May 21, 1992)

Tim Keller, *Forgive: Why Should I and How Can I?* (Penguin Books, November 27, 2023)

About the Author

Austin Gardner has been a pastor, church-planting missionary, mentor, and counselor for over fifty years, dedicating his life to serving others. A devoted husband of more than fifty years to Betty, a loving father to four wonderful children, a doting granddad to twenty grandchildren, and a great-granddad to one, Austin has forged an unwavering commitment to helping others live their best lives.

www.ingramcontent.com/pod-product-compliance
Lightning Source LLC
Chambersburg PA
CBHW071952070426
42453CB00012BA/2161